FIRST CHOICE
ONLY
CHOICE

First Choice
ONLY
CHOICE

Relationships That
Last Forever

Bill Thompson

WINEPRESS WP PUBLISHING

WinePress Publishing (PO Box 428, Enumclaw, WA 98022) functions only as book publisher. As such, the ultimate design, content, editorial accuracy, and views expressed or implied in this work are those of the author.

Unless otherwise noted, all Scriptures are taken from the *Holy Bible, New International Version®, NIV®*. Copyright © 1973, 1978, 1984 by the International Bible Society. Used by permission of Zondervan. All rights reserved.

Scripture references marked KJV are taken from the *King James Version* of the Bible.

ISBN 13: 978-1-57921-923-9
ISBN 10: 1-57921-923-3
Library of Congress Catalog Card Number: 2007932943

CONTENTS

PREFACE

Relationships are the most important part of a happy life! But unhappy people are everywhere—so why do relationships fail? And why are good relationships so hard to find? Our culture even has words for those who are expected to have dysfunctional relationships, like nerds, geeks, and so forth.

We often miss important relationship signals simply because we have not been taught what those signals are. For many years now, America has been drifting away from basic concepts about personal relationships. These principles have not been taught in our families, our churches, or our schools. As a result, we have suffered much heartbreak. We can't avoid all heartbreak, but we can prevent suffering the effects of a bad relationship. It's important to realize that our Creator had no flaws in His design for mankind, especially the plan for our relationships.

Many excellent books are available today on this subject. Most focus on how to heal troubled marriages. This book is written especially for young singles in the spirit of pre-relationship training with the hope that, with a better understanding of themselves and their intended partners, their relationships will endure with happiness.

Relationships are wonderful when they make us happy. But happy relationships can, and do, fall apart. Life becomes miserable and lonely when relationships break up. Each of us expects to have good relationships, like a best friend or a lifelong mate.

God's design for us was not flawed when it comes to bonded relationships, no matter what current divorce statistics tell us. If you Google "Divorce Statistics" on the Internet you will find web site after web site devoted to statistical data about divorce. Statistics for every state, age group and ethnic group are listed. You may conclude as I did that about half of our families are now "broken."

My generation of post-WWII baby boomers has failed miserably in forming lasting relationships. My school-age children have commented that our family life—with both biological parents still living together in one household—was not the norm. Many of their young friends are living in single-parent homes, stepparent homes, or foster-parent homes. What a great tragedy! This is a generational failure that can only be corrected by properly training the next group of couples and parents-to-be in the principles of good relationships.

Only a concerted effort to rediscover and apply the truths established by our Creator can reverse this destructive trend. Today we are living out a frightening verse of scripture: "For I, the LORD your God, am a jealous God, punishing the children for the sins of the fathers to the third and fourth generation of those who hate me" (Ex. 20:5).

So herein I will discuss relationships along with the defining words, concepts, and people. My heart's desire is to teach the next generation how to make good decisions about their relationships and the principles that must be understood to create bonds that last forever. I hope readers will discover more about themselves and engage in happy lifelong relationships without fear, because I believe people can change for the better. That is what redemption is all about.

Bill Thompson
August 2006

ACKNOWLEDGMENTS

Any book about personal relationships is a difficult work. I never expected to write about this subject, but I clearly remember when the Lord inspired me to begin writing. I asked many questions of Him and, as my understanding was enlarged, I realized I could make a difference in other people's lives by writing what I learned.

I am grateful for the encouragement of longtime friends Bob and Judy Ulrich, John and Conni Spancake, and Dick and Judy Paris, who shared much of their lives with me over many years and gave me steadfast encouragement to write. I am grateful to two young men who took their time with the manuscript and made substantive comments: my sons, James and Andrew Thompson.

Some of the material presented grew out of family devotion times around our kitchen table. My family greatly encouraged me by participating in those discussions with enthusiasm. Beth, my wife of 28 years, and our five sons—James, Daniel, Michael, Andrew and Stephen—respected my efforts and showed me that these things were of interest to teenage youth.

LOVE BY DESIGN

CHAPTER ONE

THE FIRST EVER AFTER

Eve was never alone! As she opened her eyes, the sun's morning rays warmed the man still asleep beside her. She had never seen him before, but she was not afraid. She knew instantly she could love him. It was early and above her a bird began to call its mate. Her heart started to sing also. He did not stir when she touched him. The transplant had gone well, but he had not yet come from deep, anesthetic sleep. The sunlight swept across the garden and she saw that he was bigger than she. She touched him again. This time he let out a deep breath and opened his eyes. They were brown.

WOMAN IS MOST PRECIOUS TO MAN

Eve never experienced loneliness! To every woman who longs for a bonded relationship with a man, that should be a great comfort. Eve, of course, was the first woman in the biblical account of creation. God designed from day one that man and woman should have a fulfilling but complementary relationship. The man was created first. He was given dominion over all the other creatures, with the job of naming them. He was given a pleasant garden in which to live. Then, after his career and home were established, God gave him a mate. When God noticed that there was no one to keep man company, He gave him the woman, Eve. God created the man from dust, a most humble beginning. But woman He created from the man's rib (Gen. 2:21). Why? So woman would be very precious to man!

With few exceptions, men and women were intended to keep company with someone else. But there were priorities and prerequisites. The man needed three things before he received his mate: a relationship with God, a place to live, and career responsibility. He didn't choose his own mate from among the creatures around him. God Himself made that choice and brought her to Adam.

FEARFUL AND CONFUSED

Billions of men and women now dwell on earth, each of them designed for relationship. The original design, however, has been deemed obsolete by our enlightened cultures. Broken relationships abound. Nearly half of the couples that expected to mate for life split and depart instead. Our young men and women are fearful and confused about the process of finding someone and making a commitment. So let us reexamine the fundamental design established by the Creator, place it in the context of our world and society, and learn how to establish fulfilling relationships that last a lifetime.

EVOLUTION OF THE LONELY HEART

We really cannot define love without God. Yet our modern theories of evolution and education exclude both God and creation as not relevant. The new scientific disciplines of paleo-psychology and evolutionary psychology will never comfort the lonely heart by explaining how it was formed.

We know that human males and females have different emotional "wiring." Without God's creation, these differences would have had to evolve simultaneously and compatibly in two separate creatures in order to ever produce rational offspring. The notion that two mammals (one a male, the other a female) evolved to become rational beings simultaneously (and that their offspring did not regress) is beyond an evolutionist's wildest imagination. If we even try to imagine what love would be like without God's work of creation, it becomes nonsense.

Suppose for a moment we consider the evolution of mankind instead of creation. At some point in history, give or take a million years, the DNA of a single mammal that walked upright mutated to form a rational mind. In other words, it evolved into a new species. Let's suppose it was a female of the former species. She now had thoughts and feelings, but all the males she could attract had no thoughts or feelings because the male soul had not yet evolved. They were just apes. What's a girl going to do? She would be lonely for the rest of her life. Then a million years later, a single mammal that walked upright—this time a male—mutated to form a rational mind. He was ugly, and only wanted to play ball and hunt with the other males. Sorry girls, it's going to be another million years before you get Prince Charming out of one of these monkeys. No, without God's design in creation, love makes no sense. It is absurd to think in terms of evolution when considering human relationships!

LOVE IS CREATED—ADAM MEETS EVE

The Lord God said, "It is not good for the man to be alone. I will make a helper suitable for him" (Gen. 2:18). Did Adam and Eve enjoy a perfect relationship? When Adam met Eve, the Bible says he was told to "rule over the fish of the sea and the birds of the air, over the livestock, over all the earth, and over all the creatures that move along the ground" (Gen. 1:28). Having all that authority, we might say Adam owned everything on earth at that time. He had substantial authority and job security. He had a garden apartment overlooking the Euphrates River—he was all set!

EVE MEETS ADAM

When Eve met Adam, she had no competition for his affections. She was the most beautiful woman on earth—the only woman on earth, in fact. He was all hers! There was not another woman on earth to distract him. She had no reason to doubt his perfect commitment and enduring faithfulness. He had a plan and direction for his life. Adam was delighted to see her, and spent all his time showing her around the garden and the river. It was never cold in Paradise. They bonded immediately!

NO HANDICAPS IN PARADISE

Adam and Eve had no prior broken relationships. They had no in-laws, no emotional handicaps, no debts, or preconceived notions of any kind when they started their relationship. By God's design, it was a honeymoon in Paradise. They had only each other to talk to, and were completely open with one another. Each new feeling was discovered together.

SIN RUINED EVERYTHING

But were they happy forever after? Life was good before they sinned by eating of the fruit of the forbidden tree. After the apple incident,

Adam lost the garden apartment and the dominion over all creatures. Eve knew the pain of childbirth. Heartbreak and trials were introduced into their relationship. Then their sons Cain and Abel fought to the death. Sin ruined everything. Life was no longer good.

HOW DO YOU KNOW A RELATIONSHIP WILL WORK OUT?

Generations of young men and women have longed for joyful and fulfilling relationships with high expectations. Yet they have never been trained to know the fundamental requirements for this basic human need. We are trained to cook, travel, manage money, play a musical instrument, keep house, and drive a vehicle. Then we learn how to manage a budget, file our taxes, and apply for a home mortgage. But what about how to choose and maintain a long-term bonded relationship with another person? How many hours with an instructor and textbook have you spent on that subject? Lack of training has led many people through the heartbreak of a broken relationship. Divorce is the predominant statistic, but other relationships—mother-daughter, father-son, brother-brother, and others—have also been damaged by ignorance, negligence, and sin.

So how then is the perfect relationship formed? For Adam and Eve, the process was simple. They did not choose each other, because God had only created one of each kind. They did not take marriage vows, because God himself had made the commitment. They were perfectly matched, perfectly compatible in every way.

But today we face a dilemma. For generations, we have become accustomed to choosing our own mate with little or no training or counsel in the process. We all know that "falling in love" is more like an accident than a preconceived plan. Our dilemma is how to know if we—or the soul mate we have fallen for—is ready for a lifelong relationship, and able to commit to it with integrity.

CHAPTER TWO

DESIGNED TO CONNECT

We all have relationships. They are fundamental to our lives as human beings. We were made for relationship, with body, mind, and spirit designed to connect with others. These relationships define the course of our lives for happiness or misery. But have you ever wondered what makes a relationship good or bad? Do you know how to discover a relationship that will bring a lifetime of happiness?

What, exactly, is a relationship? Webster's Dictionary says simply that it is the state of being related, like a relative or kinsman.[1] Related means connected by blood or alliance. That doesn't help, does it? It doesn't answer the burning questions about how to find permanent and fulfilling relationships, or how to find our lifelong mate, in particular.

So what does it take to make a relationship? First, you need some partnership skills. This is because you want a relationship with a person who is not wired to think and to feel like you do. Guys want a girl—and girls want a guy—who can make them happy. To be happy, you need to find someone who is a good partner for you. Partnership skills can be learned, but most young adults do it the hard way, trying different things to learn by experience what makes a good relationship. Psychotherapist Dr. Neil Clark Warren, founder of eHarmony.com, has shown that compatibility makes a difference for a happy relationship in the choice of one's partner.[2] His computerized screening procedures have been very successful in matching people for long-term happiness.

But is computer matchmaking the answer? No, not if you don't know yourself well enough to answer the survey questions about yourself, and not if you haven't learned any relationship skills. Individuals with potential relationship problems are screened out by Dr. Warren's survey questions.[3] Given the widespread loneliness and broken heart experiences in America today, I daresay all of us have potential relationship problems until we are taught what works and what doesn't work. Or we learn the hard way, and try again.

Is a good compatibility profile sufficient to ensure your happiness? Instant matchmaking plays right into one of our society's most pervasive attitudes: instant gratification in everything. The Internet matchmaking approach does for our hearts what all-night, drive-through fast food does for our bodies if we are not wise. Just as fast food requires no skill as a chef, fast matchmaking requires no skill as a partner. Instant matchmaking makes no sense without some relationship skills. It is not for teens, or even young adult singles, until they understand the skills of relating to a partner.

The pain of loneliness is real. We rush to soothe that longing. With hunger instantly satisfied, you end up with poor nutrition; when loneliness is instantly satisfied, you get poor bonding. Before you log on, fill out the survey, and receive your matching prince or princess, you must understand character assessment, faithfulness, and promises. Then you will need time together, involvement in each other's lives, commitment to meet each other's needs, forgiveness when needed and, in no small part, God's grace. If you take any of these away, you have only an incomplete recipe for relationship. The one missing element will cause heartache, or worse—breakup.

What is loneliness? Is it just the feeling of being alone? Most of us do not experience loneliness just because we are alone during a portion of our daily routine. Many people work alone, live alone, and enjoy their quiet time alone. Very busy people do not feel loneliness while they are performing whatever they do that makes them so busy. They are concentrating, striving, negotiating, performing, appealing, sweating, and rushing. They are late, in a hurry, falling behind, and exhausted, but not lonely.

Loneliness begins when we slow down and idle, when we unwind and stop striving, when we get where we are going and the performance is over. As soon as we rest, we notice that no one else is there. There is no one to share coffee, no heart-to-heart talk, no affectionate touch, no twinkling eye, no one to play with! Our families and neighbors around us do not make the deep connection we long for. We suddenly realize we have nothing to do, and no one to do it with. Nights and weekends are the worst.

We need relationships. We were designed to connect with each other in pairs as couples. But more than just connect, we were designed to bond with someone. Babies bond, best friends bond, and soul mates bond. In each stage of our life, bonding fills up the empty place we call loneliness. Each stage takes longer. Babies bond immediately with their mother and father. Best friends bond easily through shared interests, lifestyles, and ideals. But our soul mate must be searched out from a throng of candidates. During the time of searching and waiting, we are lonely. After a broken relationship ends, we start over, lonely again, with a little more wisdom about what works for us, and what doesn't.

What is the prescription for nothing to do and no one to do it with? Enlarge your life! Get off the couch and out of the house, and get busy. Volunteer! Seek out more friendships. Try a new hobby that involves other people. This get-up-and-go lifestyle will fill the void of loneliness and expose you to new people. You will be more attractive just by participating. This recommendation is not a cure, but it will help you cope with loneliness. Very busy people are not lonely until they slow down. When they fall asleep and when they awake, they feel their aloneness.

WHAT ABOUT GRACE?

Today's American society wants to teach young people about relationships to reduce teen pregnancies, fatherless children, abuse, and neglect. But government-funded studies, new educational methods, and psychological surveys cannot and will not consider the *grace* ingredient. While role-playing exercises and examples from literature provide guided experiences of relationship and responsibility, this is not sufficient. Statistics show that even with society's know-how, half of marriages actually fail. The deep understanding of how and why relationships work is only answered by the Creator of love, God Himself. Grace is God's involvement in our lives. Clearly we need help with our relationships, because so many of them break up. We need help during our time of waiting in loneliness, because we have nothing to do. We need help when our bonded relationships are in danger of breaking, because we want to make them work. And we need help to find happiness, because we can't find it by ourselves. Without a foundation of understanding relationship principles, many of your real-life experiences will be heartbreaks. Keep reading. Bonding and love are discussed next.

CHAPTER THREE

BONDING BY BLOOD, BONDING BY CHOICE

I remember the day he was born. Labor and birthing took nearly twenty-four hours . . . all day and all night. We were both exhausted. My firstborn emerged quite blue in the face from a double-wrapped cord around his neck. Doctor handed me a tiny oxygen mask to place over his face while my son looked around the room with wide-open eyes. Our bonding didn't take more than a few minutes, and it's lasted 25 years.

Special human relationships form bonds. A bond is a relationship with a deep heart-to-heart connection. It endures time and trouble. Human beings bond in universal and eternal combinations of one-to-one relationships. Some are given to us, and some we choose for ourselves. We know by experience about mother-child bonding, as well as father-son, father-daughter, brother-sister and brother-brother bonds. These are our blood relationships. They are preordained for us by God. We have no say in the choices He makes for us. Some of our blood relationships result in bonds that last a lifetime. Others become the source of embarrassment, resentment, or bitterness. You will probably experience heartbreak for the first time within your own family; in response, your bond will weaken.

Relationships outside our families are not blood relationships. They are peers, co-workers, neighbors, teachers, pastors, mentors, coaches, and others. These come and go in our lives without bonding. They are acquaintances or friends. They can add stress to our lives, but not heartbreak. People cannot cause us broken hearts if we have not bonded with them, because we do not allow them to know us intimately.

After we experience the pre-ordained blood relationships and non-bonded friendships, we then choose bonded relationships on our own. In particular, we choose a best friend, a mate for life, and a Redeemer. The choices we make determine our future happiness or heartache.

BEST FRIEND

The three types of bonds we choose are distinctly different. A best friend is neither a blood bond nor a consummated bond. But the relationship we share with our best friend is intimate, special, and long-lasting. Most of us form a best friendship relationship without getting hurt. It is one of our happiest experiences with someone else. It is an easy, stress-free choice to select a best friend. They are a lot like us: same gender, same interests, same heart's desires. We easily form that long-lasting bond.

BONDING TO ONE WITH DIFFERENT WIRING

Choosing a lifelong mate, however, is much harder than choosing a best friend. Our chosen partner is not like us in gender and has a heart that is "wired" differently. In the beginning, we really don't understand each other, but being together feels good. Attraction feels good. Affection feels good. In fact, God intended it to be so.

A mate is not a blood relationship bond, but it is consummated. *Consummated* simply means to be completed by sexual intercourse. When we choose a mate, we formally proclaim a vow of lifelong unity and fidelity. We have a marriage ceremony and celebration. We then complete the bonding by living and sleeping together. The heart-to-heart bond is very strong when we "become one flesh" (Gen. 2:24). The amazing result is the start of a new generation of God-ordained blood relationships!

BONDING WITH GOD

The third type of bonded relationship we may choose is formed with God. Many people do not want a relationship with God, but without this relationship in place, we cannot understand the purpose for human relationships. If we replace God with evolution, we may still fall in love, but because our relationships serve only our own pleasure, they will fill only a small portion of our needs. Consequently, we lack purpose and our lives feel empty, with many of our needs left unfulfilled.

The relationship we make with God gives purpose to everything that follows. Thus, the bond with our life-mate becomes stronger because our purpose is more than just pleasure. When we bond with God, both the attraction and the affection are different. They are not triggered by biochemistry, but rather by a deep-felt need within the soul of our beings. God put this need there at creation. You cannot see or hear it. But a relationship with Him answers the deepest questions about our purpose in life. Only this relationship can tell you who you are, and why God created you in the first place.

Because of the sin of Adam and Eve, we need redemption to return to the original design of relationship. Jesus Christ fills our need for redemption. Your relationship with Him gives you the understanding you need to form a bonded, consummated relationship with your lifelong mate. Only Christ-believers can receive assurance that the man or woman they have fallen in love with was truly meant for them. This is a foundational principle of long-lasting relationships! It is not found in the computerized matchmaking service.

BLOOD BOND BY CHOICE

The relationship we form with Jesus Christ as our redeemer is unique; it is a blood relationship that we choose. *His blood is substituted for ours.* That, in fact, is how our redemption works! This relationship exists between our spirits rather than our physical bodies. The consummation of the relationship takes place when His spirit fills us. That is being born again. When we grasp an understanding of this ultimate bonded relationship between us and Jesus Christ our redeemer, we can see why God used marriage in the Bible as a model of Christ and His Church.

CHAPTER FOUR

THE POWER OF INTIMACY

Some questions that beg to be answered include:

- Why do people separate after forming such a special intimate relationship?
- Why, after many years together, does bitterness take root and grow?
- How can I form an intimate relationship that will last forever?

When we bond in a relationship with another person, we allow that person to hold power and control in our lives. Friendships and acquaintances can offend us, but we get over that without deep wounds when we move on to new friendships.

Bonded relationships, however, can tear us apart emotionally. Bonding leads to intimacy, which includes an openness and transparency with one another not normally shared with everyone we meet. It is a special trust we have with one another. Intimacy develops through the sharing of one's hopes and dreams, and even the sharing of one's body. You have intimate knowledge of each other within a family, and with your best friend, but the most intimate bond forms through sexual intimacy. The more intimate the bond, the more exposed we become. We risk emotional injury if the relationship fails. The bond is even more than a heart-to-heart connection that endures. We actually become a vital part of the other person's life. Life becomes most miserable when we must live without our bonded soul mate.

The bond itself is not love, however. Misunderstandings, personal failures, and even lack of love do not break strong bonds. Love grows after bonding occurs, not the other way around. That is why we discuss bonding first. From the bond comes the decision to love. Did you get that? Love is a decision, not a feeling.

Many relationships are weak because a bond has not been formed, nor has a decision been made to love. Bonding requires some level of commitment. Feelings change. Bonds and decisions stand as true commitments. Truth has power in our lives and never changes. The truth of a bonded relationship is that our partner affects us forever.

Intimacy without the corresponding commitment and decision to love has the power to ruin our lives. The Bible discusses this in Paul's letter to the Ephesians:

> So I tell you this, and insist on it in the Lord, that you must no longer live as the Gentiles [unbelievers] do, in the futility of their thinking. They are darkened in their understanding and separated from the life of God because of the ignorance that is in them due to the hardening of their hearts. Having lost all sensitivity, they have given themselves over to sensuality so as to indulge in every kind of impurity, with a continual lust for more.
>
> (Eph. 4:17–19)

This means that a lifestyle of craving more sensuality and impurity results in loss of sensitivity, useless thinking, misunderstanding, ignorance, separation from God, and selfish stubbornness. This is not a description of living happily ever after! Bonded relationships break because hearts harden and become insensitive, and lust increases.

SIDE-BY-SIDE BONDING

Bonded relationships form due to common interests and needs. People who like each other decide to hang out together, enjoy their similarities, and form bonded relationships. A common picture of male bonding is two guys standing in front of a car with the hood up, staring at the engine. They stand side-by-side in silence, enjoying the moment. Don't forget what a car means to a guy. It is power, pride, achievement, freedom, and independence. It attracts girls! It offers adventure, speed, and thrill. They understand it. They will do the same thing next weekend. They are not in love and not interested in any deeper intimacy, but they will cherish those moments forever. That is male bonding.

FACE-TO-FACE BONDING

Girls bond with each other through their favorite activities also, the most important one being face-to-face conversation. Guys tend to bond in silence, side-by-side. It's interesting to watch a girlfriend patiently stand by while the guys stare at the car engine. She waits to be acknowledged, to have her turn to bond with her guy, not side-by-side but face-to-face. A guy is thrilled with the respect a girl shows him by allowing him to bond with his buddies first. Guys bond by simply being together. Girls bond by talking to each other. The pattern is always the same. Guy-to-girl bonding requires some of each.

FLAWS IN THE BOND, BECOMING UNGLUED

The personality flaws of each partner weaken a bonded relationship. Flaws are like cracks in a crystal. When a bonded relationship is stressed, it may break along the fault line. These flaws are not the kind of issues you can "just get over." This is the heart of our study of relationships. Why do relationships fail? Why do many marriages fail after years of being together? Why do some people have such a hard time trusting their partners? Why do people find it difficult to accept Jesus as their Redeemer? Remember, without God, love makes no sense. Love was created. Love cannot evolve. It is not made of muscle and tissue. It has greater purpose than we see on the surface. In fact, when a person forms a bonded relationship with Jesus Christ, the bond is never broken because the character of Jesus is flawless!

But our personalities have flaws. Each of us is imperfect in our selfish desires, bad habits, immature behaviors, and ignorance. In other words, we are normal men and women in need of improvement and redemption! All too often, people bond with the wrong person. Attraction, desire, and passion become strong enough to blind us to the warning signs—signs that tell us problems are likely to occur if we continue to bond with this particular person.

Bonding has consequences. You become a part of each other . . . forever! Many separated or divorced couples still have feelings for each other, even though they cannot ever live together again. Even unmarried young couples who have dated for a time feel the consequences of their bond many years later. A woman may suffer from fear that her man's first girlfriend still has a hold on his heart. Likewise, a man may find out his woman's first boyfriend has not been forgotten. Even stronger consequences come as the result of sexual behaviors like sleeping around, multiple partners, and prostitution. Your partners (all of them) become part of your emotional personality for the rest of your life! This prevents you from being completely available to your new partner.

Guilt, shame, and painful memories are all consequences of bonded relationships that we should never have entered into in the first place. These all work against the pure intimacy and openness needed when you meet the right person at the right time, and plan a forever-bonded relationship.

CHAPTER FIVE

LOVE IS . . .

We whisper "I love you" in a romantic moment to express feelings of closeness, happiness, and unity. Or we say, "I am in love with you," which means my total attention is focused on you. "You attract me, excite me, and make me happy and content." "You consume my thoughts and have my full attention." "I can't live without you." Or as spoken in the movie *Jerry McGuire,* "You complete me." These phrases signify passion, not commitment. Passion expresses feeling. We hear it in movies in the most romantic "love" scenes.

But what is love? Most young people today equate love with passion rather than commitment. The most well-known text on love in the Bible begins with, "Love is patient, love is kind," and goes on to include, "it always protects, always trusts, always hopes, always perseveres" (1 Cor. 13:4–7). These words do not describe passion, romance, or intimacy. They describe decision and friendship. Bonding forms a lasting friendship. Love decides and commits to keeping that bonded relationship intact forever. Bonding provides the happiness, while love is the security. If the friendship breaks, love will try to restore the bond.

A commitment to love takes great strength of character. The commitment to love unconditionally is a decision to bond permanently (the last of its kind) with a particular partner. That means a man will never bond by choice with another woman, and a woman will never bond by choice with another man. Each partner pledges to seek happiness in each other and no one else. Thus, a wife has feelings of insecurity if her husband looks at another woman, and a husband gets angry if his wife spends time with another man. In both cases, there is a perceived threat to the original bond.

Love means we decide to behave a certain way toward someone else. Unconditional love means we attach no strings to that decision. Unconditional love makes us feel secure. When someone says, "I love you," we really hope to hear, "I have decided to be faithful to you alone, unconditionally." When you hear words like that, you are no longer dating. You are courting, and ready to discuss long-term commitment.

Falling in love does not accurately describe what is happening emotionally between two people. We do not stumble into a decision to love. Falling describes the biochemical rush of attraction. Falling has no commitment. It cannot be stopped—it is not rational. Falling people cannot help themselves. Attraction cannot be controlled any more than a fall from a ladder can be controlled. You should not venture carelessly into places where you might fall.

Falling in love, of course, feels good. It is the fairy tale coming true. But without commitment, it will soon be over. A person is not ready for marriage if he or she still wants to enjoy the rush of a new attraction, or desires the freedom not to rule it out. This is the precipice where hearts are broken. Two people do not always move away from the edge of that cliff at the same time. She wants commitment now; he is not ready yet. Don't get your hopes up!

CHARACTER DEVELOPMENT

CHAPTER SIX

GROW UP AND CHANGE

Everyone changes. We are expected to change as we grow up. "When I was a child, I talked like a child, I thought like a child, I reasoned like a child. When I became a man, I put childish ways behind me" (1 Cor. 13:11).

The best relationships make us better people than we would otherwise be. Only in a relationship do we get a daily look in the mirror at who we are on the inside. How did I handle yesterday's criticism from my partner? Did I forgive? Did I get over it, deserved or not? Am I sulking, still angry, bitter?

Many people change for the worse. They become lazy, or they accept an attitude of defeat. They act like children. Do not enter a long-term bonded relationship like a child. A child can only bond with an adult in blood relationships, as in a father-daughter or a grandfather-grandson relationship. But relationships formed in the pre-adult years bring heartbreak if the change from child to adult is not finished in either partner. When a man seeks a bonded relationship with a girl (unfinished child), she will not be ready to meet his needs, nor will she understand him. When a boy (unfinished child) seeks a bonded relationship with a woman, he will still see her as a girl, not understanding her needs as a woman. Children view the world as their sandbox, a safe place to play. A child is content to have someone else meet his needs. An adult recognizes responsibility to take over his own provision. An adult with a renewed mind recognizes a duty to provide for the needs of someone else. This is why a relationship with Jesus Christ is vital to success in a long-term bonded relationship. It is in forming our relationship with God that our minds are renewed. In other words, we grow up! No one can meet his partner's expectations, inherent in the marriage vows, without putting childish ways behind him.

Consider the biblical account of Joseph and Mary's relationship. This couple had some unusual problems. But they handled them with grace and maturity. Mary, a young woman of child-bearing age, was betrothed to Joseph, but God had something special for her to do before she began a normal life with her husband. Mary had a supernatural visit from an angel and a supernatural conception of a child without intercourse. She had been well-trained as a Jewish girl to understand that God calls His people to special times of service, and she did not panic when called by the Lord to serve Him first. Her response was: "My soul glorifies the Lord" (Luke 1:46).

Where did this young Jewish woman get that kind of grace, all the while knowing she would endure certain humiliation for being pregnant and unmarried? If she and Joseph had picked a date, rented a hall, and invited their friends, then she would have to put it all on hold for another year, or show up as a pregnant bride. What would she tell Joseph? How could anyone believe she was pure? What a terrible start to this marriage relationship. But Mary didn't panic. She actually trusted that God knew what to do, and that He wasn't destroying her life.

Joseph had a visit from the Lord also. He didn't panic either. He had a dream wherein God told him to take Mary as his wife, and not put her away quietly as he thought to do. Joseph realized his honeymoon would not be what he had hoped for. Even though he hadn't conceived the child Mary carried, he would be the father and provider.

So Mary and Joseph became willing servants to God's greatest work, the redemption of all mankind. Their lives would never be normal again. It happened during their courtship days. Can you imagine a tougher call to service? But their marriage relationship was eventually consummated after Jesus was born. Do you think they found happiness together? Do you think they had a lot to talk about? Do you think anyone ever had pillow talk like that couple? They were together in a bonded relationship for the rest of their lives.

Could you do that? Could you change your plans to serve the Lord, if He called? "Why should I?" you may ask. Let me explain the benefits Mary and Joseph received. First, Mary's new husband was perfectly made for her by the Lord. God Himself planned this match. There were no broken or unqualified promises, no emotional handicaps. Preconceived notions, pride, and vanity were already dealt with during Mary's angelic visitation and during Joseph's dream. He was gentle and understanding. She was truthful. He was skilled in his trade of carpentry. She was pure in heart. They came from the same cultural background and training. Joseph was given a son as the firstborn child in his house. Jesus was a perfectly obedient child for His mother and father. Their home was peaceful. They were together for life. It doesn't get any better than that! Don't you want a relationship like that?

These qualities would not describe the typical home today, would they? God chose this couple very carefully because the stakes were so high. Will you allow Him to give you input on your decision to marry?

You will probably confide in someone when you think you've found your soul-mate. Before you make a commitment, ask God for His opinion, too. He is the only person who knows your future now. If you involve Him and trust His inspiration, you will most likely have a happy relationship.

Joseph and Mary were ordinary people. They were not wealthy, famous, or otherwise special in their community. God got involved in their relationship. Marriage and family life is so important to God that you can expect He will be interested in yours too, if you will ask Him.

You can begin to talk with God at any point in your life. It does not matter if you don't presently go to church, or if you don't know if you believe in Christ. Simply speak your thoughts, out loud, to Him. Ask for help with your loneliness. Ask for someone special to come into your life. Ask if the person you are with now is the right one for you. Listen with your heart as Joseph and Mary did.

CHAPTER SEVEN
WHAT'S IN YOUR CHARACTER?

Character is built like a reputation, a little at a time. It is based on decisions you make that stand the test of time. Strength of character comes from strength of your convictions. What are you willing to stand up for? To claim that everyone should do what is best for himself is to stand for nothing. This is important because you want strength of character in your relationship partner. Strength of character is the substance of commitment. Remember, you are reading this book because you want to know ahead of time why relationships fail. Why do people quit and split? Will it happen to me?

Attraction, affection, passion, and common interests are not the strengths of a bonded relationship. These are feelings, not decisions. The heart-to-heart connection's strength lies in the commitment. Character forms the substance of that commitment through the decisions you make.

Suppose you desire to find someone to love you forever with a lifelong, unwavering commitment. You can't test that person's commitment until a moment of decision arrives, but you can examine his or her character. Moreover, you can learn how to build your own character so as to attract the character traits you want in a partner.

You examine someone's character through normal conversations about significant issues. Read the news; pick any topic except the weather. Ask for an opinion. Look for conviction. Ask questions like: "Will you vote in the next election?" "Will you vote for a pro-life candidate?" "Is downloading music stealing?" "Are you offended by bedroom scenes in PG-13 movies?" Don't ask, "Will you go to church with me after we're married?" It's too easy to say yes now and procrastinate later. If your partner has no opinion about responsibility to vote, or no opinion about abortion (a topic that has divided the nation for many years), or no opinion about music downloads (an issue that has affected many college students who became targets of legal action by the music industry), or no opinion about provocative entertainment (a topic of great concern to parents), then you will have to look further to see character strength. You get the idea. If you reach the altar with this person, you will have very high expectations when the vows are spoken. Are you sure?

Strong moral character in yourself will be an essential ingredient to attract the person of your dreams. Think about issues that are important to you, and the society in which you want to make your future. Form your opinions. Make decisions. Be ready for the same kind of character inspection. Be passionately committed to some*thing* before you try passionate commitment to some*one*!

Noticing these strength of character decisions are the prelude to a decision to love. The kind of love that makes a marriage last requires an unconditional decision. Only after a person can say with conviction that he will never cheat, lie, or steal, can he also say with conviction, "I will never leave you . . . ever." Strength of character builds upon layers from easier decisions to harder ones. The kind of unconditional love that makes us feel safe with our partners is the kind we learn from God. His standards are absolute and unchanging. His love for you is unconditional. You need a personal relationship with Jesus Christ to understand how anyone can make a decision to love someone and not turn back from that decision.

If you decide to form relationships without God's training, those relationships will lack the strength of character to be long-lasting. Jesus said "I am with you always, to the very end of the age" (Matt. 28:20). Only after embracing His promise to you can you make the same promise to your spouse.

Granted, many Christian couples divorce. The strength of their commitments did not stand up under pressure. Serious problems like adultery overwhelm them. They did not promise with conviction not to cheat, and to ask for help when things got tough. But you want a better relationship than that!

CHAPTER EIGHT

THINGS YOU WISH YOU KNEW

Integrity is the first foundational principle needed to make a relationship work. Think of the scam artist; he has no integrity. He can lie with a smile, and deceive you with a handshake. Trouble comes to anyone who makes a relationship with him. Scripture says it this way:

> There is deceit in the hearts of those who plot evil.
> (Prov. 12:20)

> No one who practices deceit will dwell in my house; no one who speaks falsely will stand in my presence.
> (Ps. 101:7)

According to Webster's Dictionary, integrity is moral soundness, honesty of the whole moral character.[4]

The following story from the Bible is about a married couple who lacked integrity. The husband's pride led him to conceive a scheme of deceit. He was quickly destroyed by his lie. His wife agreed to the lie, and was destroyed shortly after her husband. She did not have good judgment about her husband's lack of integrity. Here is their story:

> Now a man named Ananias, together with his wife Sapphira, also sold a piece of property. With his wife's full knowledge he kept back part of the money for himself, but brought the rest and put it at the apostles' feet. Then Peter said, "Ananias, how is it that Satan has so filled your heart that you have lied to the Holy Spirit and have kept for yourself some of the money you received for the land? Didn't it belong to you before it was sold? And after it was sold, wasn't the money at your disposal? What made you think of doing such a thing? You have not lied to men but

to God." When Ananias heard this, he fell down and died. And great fear seized all who heard what had happened. Then the young men came forward, wrapped up his body, and carried him out and buried him.

About three hours later his wife came in, not knowing what had happened. Peter asked her, "Tell me, is this the price you and Ananias got for the land?" "Yes," she said, "that is the price." Peter said to her, "How could you agree to test the Spirit of the Lord? Look! The feet of the men who buried your husband are at the door, and they will carry you out also."

At that moment she fell down at his feet and died. Then the young men came in and, finding her dead, carried her out and buried her beside her husband.

(Acts 5:1–10)

In the very beginning of the church, the new Christians were so thankful for the gift of salvation that they sold possessions and gave the money to support the work of the church. Ananias and Sapphira were probably impressed by the joy of the givers and the prosperity of the believers. They were swept along in the excitement of the movement, and decided they too wanted to be a part of it.

There were no needy persons among them. For from time to time those who owned lands or houses sold them, brought the money from the sales and put it at the apostles' feet, and it was distributed to anyone as he had need.

(Acts 4:34–35)

Now let us look closer at the relationship between Ananias and Sapphira. They were married, so they had a bonded relationship. They possessed land of considerable value. Money from the sale was substantial enough that it could be divided between a noteworthy offering to the local church with some left over for themselves. So far, so good. But vanity and pride caused them to conceive a lie. Ananias decided to impress the community with the "sacrificial" level of his giving. He was not willing to give everything to God and place himself in a state of dependence upon God to provide his needs. He felt he needed to provide for himself and rationalized the lie. He wanted to look like a committed Christian without the heart to really be one. He simply wanted to "talk the talk."

Ananias and his wife had a close relationship. They communicated about everything. They were of like mind when Sapphira agreed wholeheartedly to the deception. Apparently, neither of them had a conscience born of the "renewing" of their minds (Rom. 12:2) to question the deception.

What happened to Ananias? God immediately exposed him as a liar. Then he dropped dead. Was he saved when he died? That's a good question.

What happened to Sapphira? Peter gave her a chance to recant her deception and speak the truth, but she also lied. Then she dropped dead, as well. Was she saved when she died?

This relationship was a tragedy! Ananias would not be dead if he had dealt with his pride in a true and humble conversion. Sapphira would not be dead if she had put God first in her life. To the rest of the world, they looked like a good couple. But the Holy Spirit of God made an example of them because they lacked integrity.

We may infer from the story that Ananias was a corrupt man. Although Sapphira received the same death sentence for her agreement in the lie, could her reason for lying be different? Was she herself corrupt, or was she in agreement with her husband because they were in a close, bonded relationship? Do you think Sapphira knew before she married Ananias that he had a prideful character? Would her life have turned out differently if she recognized that marriage to a man of corrupt character would compromise her own integrity?

Character judgment plays a vital role in the decision to enter into a commitment. The story of Ananias and Sapphira was not a marriage made in heaven. Sapphira would have been better off had she not married Ananias.

No person's character is perfect. In the next chapter, we will discuss how character develops, and how to cope with character handicaps.

CHAPTER NINE

RECOGNIZING YOUR OWN HANDICAPS

So far we have examined a good relationship (Joseph and Mary) and a bad one (Ananias and Sapphira). Although Ananias and Sapphira may have been happy together, their lack of fundamental integrity brought a tragic death to both. I call that a bad relationship.

To understand what happens in relationships, we must look at the formation of personality. We will put together what we have learned from the examples of Adam and Eve, Joseph and Mary, and Ananias and Sapphira.

The concept of personality handicaps forms the next layer of our foundation for relationships. A handicap is a part of our emotional heart that has been malformed. It has not grown properly to maturity. It predisposes the personality to become more protective of a certain part of our heart. That is, we use a handicap as an excuse for hiding, protecting, or controlling areas of personality. We do this because we fear exposing the handicapped part. In his book, *Wild at Heart*, John Eldredge uses the term "wound" to describe the injury suffered by victimization of a man or woman's heart.[5] The handicap, or wound, is a tender spot that greatly affects certain areas of our lives. We all have these tender spots in our hearts that affect our personalities.

NOT YOUR FAULT

Next to broken promises, relationships are most deeply affected by our personality handicaps. Events like the premature death of a family member (especially a parent), the divorce of parents, abuse of any kind, serious illness, poverty, or even wealth deeply affect us. Our life view is altered in a negative way. Whereas a promise involves a choice on our part to make a commitment, or to accept a commitment from someone else, an emotional handicap results from circumstances beyond our control. In other words, it is not our fault! Perhaps the most significant factor in lifelong relationships is the unrealized handicaps each of us brings with us. A personality handicap is different from a lack of understanding (which we will discuss later). The quality we call personality in each one of us developed through a complex combination of life events. Childhood training (or lack thereof), broken or intact family life, prior failed relationships, peer pressure, family values, abuse of any kind, and spiritual renewal of our minds (salvation) all play a part in forming our personality. Other people judge us and relate to us without seeing the events that formed who we are. This is especially true in relationships formed by couples attracted to each other.

On the surface, one's personality may look good, but underneath that surface are issues being hidden or protected from view. A person interacting in a relationship makes an effort to show his best qualities. We all do this naturally. It's human nature.

There are two sides to this show of personality. One side is intentional deception. This results from sin in a person's life. Ananias was such a person. Another sad example is seen in the scam artist who charms people while lying to them, cheating them, and stealing from them. Most people are not intentionally deceptive.

The other side is the fear of rejection. In the same way a person covers a skin blemish to look better, a person will cover personality flaws and handicaps to enhance their positive appeal or influence on another person. The fear of rejection makes us victims of our own handicaps. We hide or cover these issues while forming our relationships.

All of us have some personality handicaps from imperfect childhood training, peer pressure, and so forth. We get over these in time, as we mature. They are insignificant in the personalities of most adults. But more serious situations—divorced or separated parents, or abuse of any kind—are issues a person cannot just "get over." These cause serious wounds to the heart. These hurts go so deep that we have great fear of ever reopening that wound. For example, recall the recent news stories about young men who were sexually abused by Catholic priests. They could not speak out about their ordeal until many years had passed. Many waited 20 years or more to testify of their abuse.

Sadly, a large percentage of people under age 60 have lived in broken homes or been deeply affected by abuse. This means most teenagers and young single adults today have emotional handicaps that will affect their ability to find happiness in long-term bonded relationships. In short, they cannot trust intimacy. Fundamental trusts were broken. That pain affects the way they can open their hearts.

COMMITTED TO THE COMBINATION

Here is the essential issue of happy long-term bonded relationships: can two people be happy together and remain committed to each other, given the combination of personalities they bring into the relationship? Usually, when we are doing our best to attract someone, we don't discuss our known handicaps, but avoiding that discussion leads to unfulfilled expectations and unhappiness. However, by choosing to discuss your handicaps, you overcome the fear of the issue being discovered. Without such humbling confession, a budding relationship can grow no deeper.

When we choose our best friend, we are naturally drawn to people with experiences and character traits like our own. It's why we become friends in the first place. As the friendship deepens, we learn to overlook the flaws and handicaps in our friend, and they do the same for us. The bond is formed.

When we choose a lifelong mate, however, we do not discover things hidden deep in our partner's heart unless they choose to reveal them. This is because men and women are so different in emotional makeup. With your best friend, there is greater understanding because you share the same gender or emotional wiring. Women understand the heart issues of a woman. Men understand the heart issues of a man. You may not need words to understand each other. Your intended mate, however, will be just the opposite. You will not have a clue how much it hurts if the handicap of the heart is well hidden. You can reduce the stress on a relationship—and future heartache—by taking the time before marriage to be open with your fiancée about your own story, and the things that caused you hurt.

For many young men and women today, if parents divorced, the father departed. Girls no longer had the paternal protection and covering that the father was meant to provide. No stepfather or foster father could know her as well as her natural father, because God made that choice. Boys lost the first person in their lives that could validate their masculinity. Even a kind and loving stepparent could not replace the original blood relationship that God had chosen for them. A hurt and a handicap forms in a heart when the father leaves the home.

Looking back one generation, the issue of divorce was not as widespread. However, wars in Vietnam and elsewhere, careers with long hours, excessive commute times, frequent business travel, working mothers, late dinners, and fast food resulted in hurts and handicaps of neglect and loneliness. These were the "latchkey kids," as they were called, children who came home from school in the afternoons to an empty house.

Emotional handicaps and hurts are not a new phenomenon. But their scope is now more complex than ever, affecting everyone's relationships. Few couples remain happy. The idea of commitment raises either fear, or resignation to likely failure.

This chapter awakens painful feelings for many young people, I'm sure. In the next chapter we will discuss how to deal with these issues.

CHAPTER TEN

OVERCOMING HANDICAPS—CAN THIS RELATIONSHIP WORK?

There is good news at this point. One's personality handicaps can be offset by their partner's strengths. This relationship can work! Although you may not understand this clearly at the time, personality handicaps play a part in the attraction between two people in the first place. But love, not attraction, is what makes a relationship work.

Consider this list of character opposites:

- fear—courage
- impatience—patience
- boredom—contentment
- unbelief—belief
- insecurity—confidence
- undisciplined—disciplined
- low self-esteem—normal self-esteem
- weakness to temptation—self-control
- lack of motivation—self-motivation.

Each quality, whether good or bad, is a force in the formation of the relationship. Personality handicaps manifest themselves in the negative qualities, in response to painful life events.

Remember Lancelot and Guinevere in the movie *First Knight?*[26] Lancelot was absolutely fearless with a sword. He fought with abandon because he had no reason to protect his own life. He had nothing to believe in. He was a drifter. By his own admission, he lived most his life outdoors. His personality handicaps came from the tragic murder of both parents, a brutal act he witnessed as a boy. A jealous warlord destroyed his village and locked most of its citizens in the church while it burned to the ground. Lancelot was instantly orphaned. As a young man, he tried not to remember those terrible days. He grew up as a loner. He formed no relationships. His handicapped personality left him clueless about love and his purpose in life.

Lady Guinevere had lost her father. She was a young maiden, burdened with responsibility to protect her country's people after her father's death. The first meeting between Lancelot and Guinevere was violent. Lancelot grabbed her from behind and threw her to the ground to hide her from her would-be kidnappers. She hardly saw his face. It was not a normal, polite introduction. Then fearless Lancelot fought and killed the three armed men sent by the evil prince Maligant to capture the lady.

With danger diverted, they were instantly attracted to each other. But Lancelot was impatient, undisciplined, and lacking in self-control. He began to speak words of seduction. He propositioned her with immediate sexual intimacy. She was already engaged to Arthur, King of Camelot. Thus began an impossible relationship.

Prince Maligant's rogues later captured Lady Guinevere a second time. Lancelot leapt from the 50-foot-high castle wall into the moat, clung to the boat carrying her away, captured a horse, and rode to her rescue. Again they faced each other in a moment of passion during the trip home. Recognizing his indiscretion, Guinevere questioned his motives. He said to her, "Tell me what to do; I give you my life." He was absolutely lost to normal lifestyle and normal relationships. He had a major personality problem.

Guinevere became his reason to live, his reason to seek a normal lifestyle. He joined with Arthur and the knights. He found acceptance, friendship, and motivation to integrity. No longer fighting for himself alone, he fought for a cause in the battle for Lioness. So here was the match-up between Lancelot and Guinevere. Lancelot was fearless but undisciplined, with low self-esteem, weak in the face of temptation, having no self-motivation toward a destiny. Guinevere was fatherless, burdened with responsibility to protect her people, resigned to marry Arthur to provide an alliance of protection. This destiny was not her heart's desire.

Thus, each had personality handicaps from circumstances beyond their control. Her integrity and self-esteem gave him reason to live for someone beside himself. His fearless strength in battle and abandoned passion taught her to face the truth in her own heart. They both had to change. They both *did* change. In the movie, Arthur died of battle wounds, and Sir Lancelot was left to marry Lady Guinevere.

Men love this timeless story because they would like to fight valiantly to protect a beautiful woman and win her heart. Women like this story because they long to be cherished by a warrior strong enough to protect them. Lancelot and Lady Guinevere formed a strong heart-to-heart bond even with circumstantial handicaps. Even as Arthur's funeral float burned on the water, we sensed a happily-ever-after for Guinevere and Lancelot. Each overcame their issues through the strengths of the other.

Each of us would like to be described with all the positive attributes: courageous, patient, content, believing, confident, disciplined, self-controlled, self-motivated, with normal self-esteem. But in truth, none of us possess *every* positive attribute, or *only* positive attributes. When you find two people with largely the same set of personality qualities, they compete with each other rather than form an intimate relationship.

What is attraction? Attraction is part personality, part unspoken invitation, part biochemistry, part mutual interest, all at the right time and place. Why do we need someone? We sense a longing for companionship to fill an empty part of our lives.

This mix of attraction and need blend together to form a relationship. One who is attracted to another but who feels no need for a bond is not interested in commitment, like Lancelot in his lifestyle with no roots and no home. That relationship will not move on to the next level. On the other hand, one seeking to fill a need in his life through a relationship is less concerned with the attraction, and will accept a lower standard of biochemistry or mutual interest in order to fill the need. You can see this in Lady Guinevere's acceptance of Arthur's proposal. If you doubt this, ask a couple where one or both are married for the second time.

Both Lancelot and Guinevere had lost their role models for happy relationships. Through tragic circumstances, they lost their parents' guidance. Today our young adults are also missing proper role models. As they approach the time to form lifelong bonded relationships, they see unhappiness in their parents' relationships and others around them. Their pastors, teachers, friends, and relatives are all struggling with their own relationship disappointments and heartaches.

So how do all the personality strengths and weaknesses counterbalance each other for a successful and happy relationship? The Bible says, "Perfect love drives out fear" (1 John 4:18). While it is true that only God's love is perfect, our love for one another has a redemptive quality even in its imperfect state. Thus, to some degree, one person's love for another can counterbalance another's personality handicaps. This is not romance, but it makes great relationships. It is a conscious decision to constantly forgive, continually overlook, and always protect one another in the bonded relationship. It is the self-sacrificing love of one best friend for the other, and one spouse for the other. It is the fulfillment of the marriage vow. It is the way God intended long-term bonded relationships to work!

PROMISES

CHAPTER ELEVEN
MAKE A PROMISE

Before we venture too far into emotional territory, we must look at the defining words of promise. Certain words characterize different classes of promises. These words are all about commitment. We need to understand the definitions because we depend upon promises in relationships. Broken relationships often result from broken promises. We begin with a look at promises and contracts, and progress to oaths and vows.

PROMISE

> I am with you always, to the very end of the age.
> (Matt. 28:20)

A promise is defined as:

> A declaration written or verbal made by one person to another, which binds the person who makes it, either in honor, conscience or law, to do or forbear a certain act specified; a declaration which gives to the person to whom it is made a right to expect or to claim the performance or forbearance of the act.[7]

Every child is taught what it means to make a promise. In that elementary lesson, the promise was probably understood to be verbal. But looking at the definition from Webster's, we see more emotionally complex words like *binds, expect,* and *claim.* We may wonder: Can binding lead to bondage? Does expect lead to differences of expectations? Does claim lead to control?

For some of you reading this, the definition of promise has already awakened some deep feelings. You suddenly realize that you must accept a promise from another person as the basis of a lifelong committed relationship in marriage. Does it frighten you to realize that your ability to judge a person's character is the primary prerequisite to have faith in a promise offered? This is where the phrase "love is blind" correctly describes the acceptance of a promise from one who is not qualified to make it.

I've jumped way ahead in that last statement! We have much more foundation to cover. But even if you read no further, you can now understand how a relationship based on a promise can become a heartbreak of misunderstandings.

What kind of promises should a man make? A man's role as protector and provider requires of him a promise to love, a promise to work, a promise to cover and protect, and a promise never to leave his mate. Those promises give a woman the feeling of security. No woman leaves a man who makes good on such promises!

What kind of promises should a woman make? A woman's role as one who nurtures requires of her a promise to respect, a promise to care for their home, a promise to feed, and a promise to be there for him as a friend, companion, and lover. Those promises give a man a feeling of fulfillment and roots. No man leaves a woman who makes good on such promises!

CONTRACT

A contract is a promise formalized in a written document. A contract requires legal age, freedom from coercion, and a history of integrity, like a credit report. A contract often describes an agreement to buy or sell, and is concerned with money. A well-written contract document uses precise words chosen to convey exact scope, meaning, and timeframe. A legal expert is often consulted. Whereas a promise is usually made between two people who have some level of personal trust in their relationship, a contract is commonly used to define an agreement between people who have no personal relationship. An example is a contract to buy a new car. Each person in the agreement places their trust in the written signature of the other and in the legal system with jurisdiction over such things.

One type of contract you hear about in the context of personal relationships is the prenuptial agreement. It's all about money! Trust is not relevant. Lifelong commitment is not expected. Do you think a prenuptial contract belongs among the foundational tenets of a happy relationship? Of course not! It is an excuse for not sharing. It's an excuse for withholding unconditional love and respect. The contract raises love of money above unconditional love of the person. The pre-nup is a risk mitigation plan for a short-term, less-than-lifelong commitment. It is based on fear of failure rather than commitment.

The consequence of failure to keep a contract is handled in a court of law where a judge makes the binding decision. Note the word *binding*. Failure to meet the terms of the contract becomes bondage for the parties to the agreement, and an unhappy ending.

Oath

> "I swear by Almighty God that the evidence I give shall be the truth, the whole truth, and nothing but the truth."[8]

An oath is defined as

> "A solemn affirmation or declaration, made with an appeal to God for the truth of what is affirmed; the act of calling on God to witness the truth of what is being said."[9]

An oath often accompanies a promise. Both are verbal, but an oath is witnessed. In other words, an oath is spoken before an audience that bears witness to the statements or promises. In a court of law, jurors and witnesses take a verbal oath to tell the truth. In government, the President takes the oath of office, a promissory oath.

An oath is a statement of relationship from one individual to an audience. It is not normally used in a personal relationship. Failure to keep an oath results in loss of confidence by the group of witnesses.

Vow

> I,___, take you ___, to be my wife/husband, to have and to hold from this day forward, for better or for worse, for richer, for poorer, in sickness and in health, to love and to cherish; from this day forward until death do us part.[10]

Webster's Dictionary defines a vow as:

> "A solemn promise; an engagement solemnly entered into; in a more special sense, a kind of promissory oath made to God, or to some deity, to perform some act or to dedicate

to the deity something of value on the fulfillment of certain conditions, or in the event of receiving something specially desired, such as success in an enterprise, deliverance from danger, recovery from sickness, etc.; a promise to follow out some line of conduct, or to consecrate or devote oneself wholly or in part for a longer or shorter time to some act or service; a pledge of love or devotion; as a marriage vow."[11]

A vow is a solemn promise, made with an appeal to God in the company of witnesses. In a marriage ceremony, vows are combined with a written contract bearing two witnesses' signatures on the document. The taking of a marriage vow usually includes pastoral counseling over a period of time, allowing for a comprehensive understanding of the commitment. Marriage vows combine promise, oath, and contract all together. Marriage vows are the most important promises people ever make. They are vital to the stability of our society and to our personal happiness. That is why divorce is such a tragedy.

BETROTHAL

"I will betroth you to me forever."

(Hosea 2:19 KJV)

Betrothal is another word worthy of discussion. Betrothal is such a beautiful word. It speaks of gallant courtship (imagine a knight and his princess). It means "to contract to any one, with a view to a future marriage; to promise or to pledge to be the future spouse of another."[12] Betrothal is rarely spoken of today, but listen to this passage from the Bible: "I will betroth you to me forever; I will betroth you in righteousness, and justice, and love, and compassion. I will betroth you in faithfulness" (Hosea 2:19–20 KJV).

Betrothal speaks of a perfect relationship. There is no better promise one person can give another than to offer the promise of betrothal. It takes great integrity of character to speak such words. Betroth comes from the root word *troth*, meaning "truth." All of these words—promise, contract, oath, vow, and betrothal—convey commitment. We must understand them to realize the significance of commitments offered to us by others, especially those we love.

CHAPTER TWELVE

MAJOR COMMITMENT—MAJOR RISK

His T-shirt read "No Fear." It was his teen-age maxim on a well-worn sleeveless T-shirt. He still liked the shirt, but getting respect now was not so easy. She wanted him to commit—like forever. She was beautiful. When she dressed hot, she could take his breath away. Deep down he knew this was a matter of respect. He just wasn't sure he was ready. What if he meets someone else? What if she has expectations? What if she meets someone else? How long would she wait? Commitment demands a promise.

WE NEED COMMITMENT

Bonded relationships require commitment. Commitment results in intimacy, and human beings long for intimacy. In his best selling book, *I Kissed Dating Goodbye,* Josh Harris says, "The joy of intimacy is the reward of commitment."[13] Notice that commitment must come first. Many first-time relationships get this backwards. Both young men and young women think intimacy is trial commitment. They believe emotional and sexual intimacy is the test to see if further commitment would be a good idea. They call it taking the relationship to the next level. But intimacy without commitment first does not lead to deeper love. It only leads to unsatisfied desire. Without a man's lifetime commitment, a woman's need for security goes unfilled. Without a woman's lifetime commitment, a man's need for a home with roots is never met. Commitment gives both partners a reason to come home every night. Intimacy is not necessary on a constant basis, but commitment is! Through love and intimacy, our bonded partner fulfills our needs and we fulfill the needs of our bonded partner.

Commitments are much harder to keep than they are to make in the first place. We are painfully aware of people close to us who have not kept their commitments. You know you need a bonded relation-ship with someone, but what about all these broken relationships you hear about daily?

KNOW YOURSELF

To make a commitment requires three skills. First, you must know yourself. Do you have the strength of character and integrity to com-mit for the long-term? In other words, are you a man or woman of your word? Second, you must have the maturity, training, and experi-ence to evaluate a person's promise of commitment to you. Third, you must be able to adapt to change in yourself and your partner.

You learn about yourself from others. When you are lost, for ex-ample, you ask for directions. But how many guys ask for directions? You need to get frank opinions from others about yourself regarding commitment. A guy unwilling to discuss his personal readiness for long-term commitment is not ready for the changes that will take place in himself and his partner. Those who refuse to ask for help are at high risk of not keeping long-term commitments. Hint: to make a relationship successful, ask for help. Rugged individualism does not build integrity of character.

Our reactions to those around us during life's unexpected events show our integrity of character. Integrity is a history of your charac-ter. Any man can keep his word when things are going according to plan. But when things go wrong, can you take the blame, admit your faults, ask for forgiveness, promise to improve, make peace, and live with it?

Girls, you should be concerned if your guy does not counsel with anyone during the pre-engagement phase of your relationship. If he has not learned to ask for directions yet, you will have to endure his mistakes later while he learns the timeliness of asking for help. Remember how you felt when your father got lost on family trips and insisted he knew where he was? Your mother suggested they pull over and ask someone, but your father insisted he could find the way. You will relive that frustration again and again. Are you OK with that? Love speaks up!

Guys, you must learn how to ask for and receive help. Life will not lack opportunities for you to make command decisions, overcome major obstacles, and achieve goals. But why frustrate those around you while you prove you know where you are? Love speaks up! Ask for directions. Accept the fact that relationship decisions are not easy and you don't have all the answers. Sometimes winning is all about the questions. Skill is irrelevant if you don't have all the facts.

EVALUATE THE PROMISE

The second required skill is the ability to evaluate another person's promise to you. In love, we believe everything. We see only good, and are blinded to the bad or inconsistent. But love is not just the wind of our emotions. Love is a decision you live with, not a feeling of euphoria. There may be obvious inconsistencies when someone makes a promise to us. We will examine this in much more detail in later chapters. Right now, just consider your own opinion about your partner's ability to make a promise and keep it. The biblical foundation for right motivations comes from a transformed mind. "Do not conform any longer to the pattern of this world, but be transformed by the renewing of your mind" (Romans 12:2). Above all else, this is what you want in a partner: a renewed mind. Without this transformation in character, you and your partner will follow the pattern in the world today and have only a 50-50 chance of a long-term bonded relationship with each other. That Bible verse goes on to say, "Then you will be able to test and approve what God's will is—his good, pleasing and perfect will" (Romans 12:2). With a renewed mind not conformed to the world's ways, you have a much better foundation upon which to grow a lasting happy relationship.

During your time together, listen to each other. Do you hear the words of one with a transformed character, who is motivated by integrity, seeking to know the truth, and to do what is right? Or do you hear words that sound vain, self-centered, prideful, entitled, or lazy? In the latter case, you can break up now, or break up later. It isn't going to work. Don't form the bond. Do not commit yourself to that person. This is how you evaluate his or her ability to keep a promise, a marriage vow.

ADAPT TO CHANGE

The third requirement of commitment is the ability to adapt to change. He will get grey hair, she will lose her size 2 figure, you will meet new friends, take up new hobbies, have some health problems, and so on. Highly motivated people take these changes in stride and make changes for the better. They adapt to change gracefully, even unexpected change. Motivated individuals are driven by integrity, love, trust, and a desire to finish well. Their integrity drives them to do it right. Their love drives them to make it work. Their trust drives them to be steadfast to one who is trustworthy. Their desire to finish well drives them to accomplish what was begun. If your mate is one of these motivated people, your relationship can grow and flow with life's changes. Motivation must be Christ-centered. The pairing of two highly motivated individuals is a strong, unbreakable relationship.

Unmotivated individuals will most likely change for the worse. They are not driven by anything. In time, they will become lazy, uncooperative, self-centered, and boring. If your mate becomes unmotivated, these changes will challenge your commitment. This type of person will become a greater challenge to love as time passes. The effort of commitment will increase, while happiness wanes. Your commitment integrity will be tested. The commitment that was easy to make in love will be maintained only with a decision to fulfill your word. It's much harder, but that is what it takes to make lifelong commitments work.

RISK IS RATIONAL

Risk and fear are the first things that come to mind when young men and women consider their first significant commitments in life. This is normal caution for people of integrity. Indeed, to have no fear and assess no risk is a prelude to an unhappy life. But no one can control every aspect of his life. No one can make a long-term commitment with full knowledge of the journey beforehand. So we accept the risks and suppress the fears to enter into the relationship commitment.

We evaluate risk—the chance of exposure to injury or loss—logically or rationally. We buy auto insurance, for example, because it financially covers the risk of an accident or disaster. So in our rational, pre-commitment relationship risk assessment, we ask ourselves: Can I/we afford a house? Am I willing to live where he/she wants to live? Will his/her in-laws drive me crazy? You must reconcile all the issues that come up. Compromise is OK.

Risk can be managed through open communication. The communication will dispel some risks, but may introduce others, which is why counseling is recommended prior to any major decision. For example, an attorney and financial advisor are usually consulted before closing a 30-year mortgage. Likewise, a relationship counselor such as a pastor or minister should be consulted before committing to a lifelong bonded relationship by marriage.

Courtship involves accountability. In prior generations, that was common sense. But now that we can apply for a mortgage and a mate on the Internet, I expect the results may be even worse unless counselors are consulted.

FEAR IS FEELING

Fear is the feeling we have when we don't know what will happen, and we don't know the risks. Can you remember that feeling as a child in school just before a fire drill? They tell you the alarms will sound shortly and you wait with increasing adrenaline. Then the alarm sounds, the big adrenaline rush comes, and you react as you have been trained to do. Even though we know what to expect, the sudden, loud alarm buzzer is startling.

Fear evokes in us panic, dread, alarm, trepidation, and hesitation. These words describe the same feeling to a greater or lesser degree. Whereas risk deals with facts, fear deals with feelings. We ask ourselves: Will he/she love me if I put on weight? What if I meet someone I like better? These feelings of doubt must be dealt with, and may be soothed by assurances from our partner. Courage overcomes fear only after a season produces wisdom. Character integrity requires that "seasoning." Thus, when one person makes a proposal of commitment to another, each must assess the other's ability to perform to the expectations of the commitment. We will discuss how to make this assessment in the next chapter.

ADAPTATION, MOTIVATION, INTEGRITY

Let's make our first attempt to answer the question, "Why do bonded relationships (marriages) break up?" There is no one simple answer, but so far we can see that a person's inability to handle change, lack of motivation, or lack of integrity will definitely weigh heavily during times of strife. Maybe what you perceived as love was not decision-based, but was just a romantic feeling. Maybe your partner was not ready to commit, but did anyway. Maybe the bond was not protected when someone else came along.

This book will ask that question again and again in different contexts. By exploring the issues and asking the questions in different ways, we gain satisfying insight about causes of relationship failure.

The context of this chapter is the risk of change for the worse. Changes inevitably come. Unexpected events like sudden debt, car accident, transmission failure, sudden illness, irresponsibility, or the return of a former boyfriend or girlfriend can cause strife, bitterness, anger, resentment, rejection, and neglect. A couple with these emotions can't stand to live together if they haven't planned to get help to manage these unhappy changes. Immaturities, disagreements, selfishness, boredom, and other types of character flaws drive two people apart.

Unconditional love, however, lasts forever. No matter what happens or what your mate does, love that lasts is not based on feeling or performance, but on a promise! The promise makes it work.

CHAPTER THIRTEEN
FLAWED PROMISES

So far we have defined promises, but only raised questions about the binding, the expectations, and the claims. Is it possible that the words heard when a promise was proclaimed meant something different to the one who promised? This is a misunderstood promise. It will cause heartache, because its expectations will never be fulfilled.

Promises, contracts, oaths, and vows can all be flawed by lack of maturity or understanding. A flawed promise may be made with integrity by a person who does not have the knowledge or resources to fulfill the commitment. The promise may be accepted as genuine by one who does not understand the maturity level of the promise maker. But the promise-maker may not be qualified to make the promise.

Suppose a young man without a skill and without a job promises a young woman a house after they marry. He is not qualified to make that kind of promise while he is unemployed. He is being presumptuous or, perhaps, reckless or arrogant.

Suppose a young woman with a career promises a young man that she will leave her job to go wherever his career leads him so they can be together. To make that promise, she must be willing to actually quit her job, lose her benefits, live on less money, interrupt her career, and be unemployed for a time. That's a big jump! Is she being presumptuous or reckless? What if her boss offers her more money and a promotion not to leave? Will she waver? Such a promise should not be made lightly.

In either case, the relationship does not meet the expectations of one person or the other. This is not necessarily intentional deception. It may be immaturity, lack of wisdom, or lack of counsel. This is where parents, pastors, friends, and counselors all should be heard when considering a lifelong commitment. But they don't know what you don't tell them! Of course, many parents, pastors, friends, and counselors are also clueless to discern character flaws. But that is why you are reading this, isn't it?

One unfortunate statistic about the generation of post-WWII "baby boomers" is that a very high percentage (50%) of their marriages failed and ended in divorce. Some relationships were clearly a means of escape and not a proper union. These are now the parents, pastors, and counselors who lack the wisdom to warn their grown children about the character flaws observed in the potential spouses their children bring home. For the most part, the older generation is afraid to speak up and discuss the warning signs. The younger generation thinks, of course, that the parents aren't in touch with the realities of life today. Hence there is urgent need for parents and their grown children to share thoughts with each other about potential mates.

CHAPTER FOURTEEN

BROKEN PROMISES

Promises may be misunderstood, and promises may be made by unqualified people. What about broken promises?

Some promises just cannot be fulfilled. Even with the best of intentions and integrity, people sometimes fail to meet their commitments. In a relationship, this is a big disappointment. Some promised things never get started, some never get finished, some require fundamental changes in a person's behavior, and some promises were just too big to fulfill. Every person who promises something must carefully count the cost to fulfill the promise. Promises usually involve cost in terms of money, time, or personal change.

Broken promises may have different timelines in each person's mind. The one to whom the promise is made may have the expectation of fulfillment now. The one who made the promise may have intended fulfillment some time in the future. The unspoken timeline of the promise may lead to trouble in a relationship.

Failure to keep a promise devastates a relationship. Each person in the relationship must be clear about the other's ability to make the promise. For example, if I promised you I would lift 500 pounds in a single lift, once a week, for the rest of my life to show my love for you, you would be skeptical. Would you be breathlessly swept off your feet? No, you would not! My example sounds ridiculous, of course. You would be wise not to enter into a relationship based on such a promise. So now do you feel more confident if I promise never to desire another person as long as you and I both live? What is it that convinces you that I can keep that promise? We will explore this idea in more depth later. For now, we just need to define the words.

Suppose you know the integrity of my character, and you know I work out weekly in a gym where I practice lifting weights. Why don't you feel more confident in my promise to lift 500 pounds? Because few men on earth can lift 500 pounds! Common sense suggests that promise has a high risk of being broken.

HEART TROUBLE

CHAPTER FIFTEEN

THE STOLEN HEART— LOST EXPECTATIONS

Whathat have you done? No one would say a crime has been committed. The thief himself, while proud of his adventure, does not know the significance of his deed. But there is a victim, wounded and hurting. Innocence gives way to bitterness and trust is lost. A stolen heart can never be returned!

A woman's heart is stolen when her expectations in a relationship are falsely built up by a man's words of love and promise. She allows her heart to be taken in by his idle words. Expectations can be built up and manipulated with merely the allusion of promise or commitment. To proclaim to friends that you are "going steady" or "dating" is an allusion of commitment. Such words instill specific expectations in the mind and heart of the one who hears them.

A stolen heart is often given away too easily. It is foolishness to give away too much too soon. As romantic as it sounds, heartbreak looms. It is the beginning of a relationship in trouble. The excitement of a relationship moving to the next level is irresistible, like a storybook fairy tale. While the princess longs to be swept away, the prince is not prepared for the ever–after clause. A stolen heart may be soothed by a promise of a more committed relationship in the future. Taking the relationship "to the next level" without a commitment may seem like a very romantic moment. It doesn't hurt until hope fades because the desired commitment never comes. What's wrong with this picture?

What's wrong is that the protector of the woman's heart is missing. In the story of Adam and Eve in the garden, Eve got into trouble when the serpent built up her expectations, contradicting God's command. Eve's heart was stolen by the guile of the serpent that deceived her. The allure of moving to the next level of existence, where "you will be like God" (Gen. 3:5), was irresistible. This story from the book of Genesis is called the Fall of Man, not only because Eve ate forbidden fruit, but also because her husband failed to protect her more vulnerable heart. In the Genesis account, God appeared on the scene and called the man to accountability first.

In God's design for relationships, a father's covering protection would protect a young maiden's heart from being stolen. His watchful eye and nearby presence could detect a young man's foolish words or premature promises. Recall the fact that Eve was never alone from the moment of her birth. Her Creator was not making a statement that she was irresponsible, but rather that her heart was vulnerable.

Today, however, young women routinely spend time alone with their boyfriends. Because so many fathers have separated from their families, their daughters do not have the covering of protection they need by design. Even with the best of intentions, single moms are not designed to be their daughter's covering. Those fathers who are at home have not been trained in their responsibility in this area. What's more, the young women of today have been, for more than a generation, under the influence of feminism, making them more independent than ever. The concept of courtship, in which a young man asks the father's permission to date his daughter, has been all but discarded.

It would be unfair to characterize all young men as heart-stealers. Many boys are so inexperienced in their relationship skills that their infatuations of foolish and extravagant passion are, in fact, causing the princesses in their lives to form premature expectations of happily-ever-after commitment. Just as the lives of many young women lack the umbrella of protection, the young men have not been trained in manhood and integrity. Courtship calls fathers to step up to their responsibility while the young men learn accountability for their integrity in relationship.

I recently spoke to a father with two daughters. He related the thrill he experienced when his oldest daughter's boyfriend called long distance to ask permission to court her. Father and son-in-law have become good friends as a result. The daughter was never without protection during her transition from father's home to husband's home. You can see the happiness on the faces of that young couple.

When a man speaks of his stolen heart, he does not mean he has been lured into expectations. Men (as hunters/pursuers) are not vulnerable in that way. A man's stolen heart acknowledges that he must seriously consider commitment to the princess who so enthralls and captivates him, or else he will lose her to another hunter.

Stealing a heart is an immature act that hurts the other party. It is not a happy or joyful realization to discover your expectations were aimed too high. It is an accident caused by a well-meaning but untrained young man who has spoken foolish, untimely words. Is it not the same accident as falling in love in the first place? If commitment does not follow, heartbreak surely will. Then both boy or man and girl or woman will be wounded with a personality-affecting relationship handicap, making it more difficult to trust in the next relationship.

The stolen heart becomes a lost freedom when a true and proper relationship forms. A person's heart should never be taken or given before real commitment is made. Having control of another's heart is intimacy before commitment! A stolen heart means intimacy of the soul has been taken before its proper time by false expectations, leading to feelings completely exposed.

Just as a young man does not understand the impact of his words on a woman's heart, the woman does not understand the power of her body image or her looks on his heart. This is not a place for experimentation. Boundaries must be in place to allow long-term bonded relationships to form. For every young couple, this is unfamiliar territory. Courtship provides safety when desiring more than a casual friendship. In courtship, you are not alone. Accountability and counsel are expected and provided. You receive protection from life's most painful mistakes.

But what if the father of the woman, her protector, is missing in action? Whose covering is she under? What man will serve as her protector until the transition to her husband's home? Her next larger covering is her local church. Several chapters ago, we emphasized the importance of choosing to form a relationship with God. Here is where you need it.

Because so many men have split with their wives, nearly half statistically, their sons and daughters are left uncovered and unprotected at the time when they need their fathers the most. Help is needed to break the generational curse that so easily repeats. You can find that help by becoming part of a new and larger family! In your relationship with God, He will lead you to the right church. He will show you a youth group which teaches proper relationship principles. He will connect you with a pastor and adult friends who care about your happiness. The Bible says, "The steps of a good man [or woman] are ordered by the Lord" (Ps. 37:23 KJV). *You* take the steps, and *He* will guide you to the right place. This is certainly a better risk to take than the trials and errors of relationship by experimentation.

CHAPTER SIXTEEN

THE BROKEN HEART— LOST TRUST

It was a different kind of pain! Shallow breaths, tight abdomen, dry mouth—just unending, steady pain. He would have screamed, but that could not soothe it. No prescription would have any effect. Nothing would cause it to let up. No one could help. Day and night, the ache continued, consuming all his energy and will to move on.

She had walked out—suddenly, unexpectedly, totally. Life had ended, but he wasn't dead. After dawn, the pain was manageable. It could be ignored for a while with busy-ness. But after dark, the grip of the feeling returned with agony. It was a broken heart, a wound from the inside out! The pain was only visible in his eyes. While the wound was fresh, it seemed like no healing could ever overcome it. The bond had been torn in two so quickly that the flesh was jagged.

With a strange inner assurance, he knew this pain would end, but not yet. How could he have been so blind to the increasing separation? Why was he not good enough? Honesty, faithfulness, integrity, even love had failed. Vows were shattered . . . memories erased . . . no second chance. Was it even real?

Yes, it is real. Many of you could add your own description of pain to this story because you, too, have walked there. When life events cause serious emotional hurt, there is a long-term effect on our ability to form new relationships. It is as if we grow scar tissue over one area of our heart. The healing is never absolutely perfect in its restoration of the injured area. Even long after the pain has subsided, a scar remains as a reminder of the injury. We know it is there, but the new person with whom we are forming a relationship cannot see it.

In contrast, a visible scar on a person's face will eventually evoke a question like, "What happened to you?" or "How did you injure your face?" The relationship will proceed with new understanding once that question has been discussed.

An emotional scar on one's heart, however, may be hidden from view for a long time, or even never revealed in a relationship. This means an important part of our life story remains hidden. The hidden injury still has an effect, however, as we favor the area with unusual protection. One who has suffered a broken heart is more guarded about trusting another partner. Thus, as a relationship progresses toward fuller and deeper understanding, one with an old wound to the heart is afraid to show it. There is always an element of fear in any new relationship. But fear disables love. You can never trust someone while you fear disclosure. Fear of disclosing the scar on one's heart results in low self-esteem. Ultimately, it disables an appropriately passionate response in the fulfillment of the relationship. Fear takes control of freedom.

The Bible compares the bonded relationship of husband and wife to the relationship between Jesus Christ and His bride, the church (Rev. 19:7). The bride-and-groom symbolism is significant. During our lives as mortals, we must learn the skills we will use for our immortal lives in eternity. Jesus Christ expects a passionate relationship with His redeemed bride with full disclosure (1 John 3:2). We will see Him face to face. That is one facet of His glory, to be completely embraced by His redeemed creation that chooses Him with a free will. Our greatest hope is to see Him as He is, with full disclosure between us and our Redeemer (1 Cor. 13:12). That special relationship cannot be fulfilled until all fear is overcome.

Thus, both our relationship with our mate, as well as our relationship with Jesus Christ, our Redeemer, is handicapped by the effects of broken promises. The broken heart experience is not required during the passage to lifelong bonded relationship. But today's relationships—formed without a foundation of wisdom and character—are so fragile, the broken heart wound is a common handicap. I can assure you the pain does end. Healing comes and trust returns, but help along the way is needed.

CHAPTER SEVENTEEN

THE HARDENED HEART—BITTERNESS AND RESENTMENT

A hardened heart also damages relationships. Whereas a broken heart hopes, even longs, for a healing of the wound, the hardened heart withholds forgiveness. Both are victims, but hardening forms as a defensive wall gets built upon bitterness and resentment. Bitterness is disgust, contempt, hatred. Bitterness vows never to go back. Resentment is self-centered indignation. Resentment disallows all guilt. Together, bitterness and resentment enslave a heart once free. They become like an addictive painkiller that cannot heal. They must be applied again and again over the wound.

The victim with a hardened heart resolves never to lose control and open his heart in a vulnerable way again. One with a hardened heart does not believe the wounds can ever be healed, and will not risk lowering defenses to form a new relationship. These are characteristics of an unregenerate heart, still living with guilt. Every victim of a broken relationship believes in some small way they bear some responsibility. The hardness must be softened before a new relationship can be formed.

An individual with a hardened heart cannot form a true bonded relationship because the heart is buried behind layers of protection. Any relationship formed cannot progress to intimate levels. No commitment can be chanced.

An inability to forgive signals the presence of a hardened heart. This sinful character trait requires redemption before a bonded relationship can be formed. The individual with a hardened heart cannot engage in an open trusting relationship. Unlike the brokenhearted person who clings to hope, the hard-hearted person remains without hope. The hardening will not allow it.

But God did not intend things to end that way. The bitterness, resentment, need to control, and fear of openness can be healed, but not through another human relationship. A relationship with God is needed first! Remember, God created love. If love evolved, we could take vitamins or other man-made treatments to heal and restore heart troubles. We could even hope to evolve our way out of loneliness.

Redemption of a person through belief in Jesus Christ promises heart healing now, as well as the forgiveness of sins in the past. In the Old Testament book of Isaiah, a familiar passage about Jesus' purpose says He was sent "to bind up the brokenhearted, to proclaim freedom for the captives and release from darkness for the prisoners" (Isaiah 61:1). Isn't this just what a person whose heart is hardened needs to hear? The hard-hearted one is a captive to fear of being victimized again. The healing power of Jesus Christ provides the only hope that can make a difference for such an individual.

Here is how that healing works: A hard-hearted person knows he can never trust a relationship with another person who has issues of her own. And everyone has issues. One may gossip, another may belittle, and another may misunderstand. No one can be trusted to understand. Any new relationship may cause more pain. Exposing hurts to another person, laying open the heart, and accepting help will never take place. It simply cannot be risked by a heart already wounded and hardened.

Jesus Christ, however, has never had a failed relationship. He has forgiven those who betrayed Him, mocked Him, spit upon Him, and crucified Him. He has shown love to all. He has no issues to worry about. His character is flawless. His forgiveness is forever. He waits patiently for anyone to ask Him for help. He has never betrayed a trust. And He can be approached, privately and alone. No one on earth can be trusted, but Jesus is different. He does not gossip, belittle, or misunderstand. He is not seen or heard, but He answers in the heart, where the hurt is. The hardened heart requires just enough courage to scream for help, and just enough faith to ask it of Jesus. You can do this alone. You have nothing to lose. If you don't believe in God, then you will be no worse off. And if you think He just might be real but have never gotten this close, then give it a try. That cry for help breaks a crack in the hardness of your wall. Cry out again and confess your bitterness. Another crack forms. Bitterness flows out through those cracks in your protective wall. You will actually feel it!

It is a most amazing fact of life that the God who created you finds your heart-cry for help irresistible. He will answer in a way that is personal to you. He will wait your entire life just to hear your voice speak directly to Him. As your bitterness flows out, your victim's heart is softened and hope returns.

He has done this for me, personally. After my wife of three years walked out with no discussion, I felt the pain of hopelessness, rejection, and total loss. I knew she was not coming back. My heart was completely crushed. The emptiness felt hopeless. A friend gave me a small book called *Power in Praise*[14] by an Army chaplain named Merlin Carothers. In that book, Chaplain Carothers asked me to praise God for every facet of my life, both good and bad. At that moment, it was all bad. I read on, and he continued with that theme: to praise God for everything about my life.

Alone in my apartment, I began to speak out loud to God. I was broken to tears, but I praised God for the life I had at that moment, with the pain included. No sooner had I spoken the words when the feeling of being physically drained of sorrow swept over me. As if the plug had been pulled in a tub of water, the deep hurts swirled away down the drain. I was then refilled—in the same place where the sorrow had been—with a feeling of joy, and the absolute certainty that God had heard me speak to Him from my broken heart. He answered me with healing and filling. He was alive and nearby. I was stunned to realize I had spoken to God and He had answered me. He cared. He showed up. He had an answer to my pain.

If you are suffering with the pain of a broken heart, or the bitterness of a hardened heart, I can tell you with all assurance that whether it is your fault or not, God has a way to heal you! You can be restored to find new and wholesome relationships, if you go to Him first.

Remember, Jesus never expressed bitterness or resentment against His torturers. His dying words were words of forgiveness. He spoke those words once and was done with it. Forgiveness was completed.

TRUST AND HAPPINESS

CHAPTER EIGHTEEN

THE OPEN HEART— TRUSTING A PARTNER

Relationship is a partnership. You need trust and openness to make it work. When you trust another person, you give up some of your own control. But if you must be in control—whether from fear or pride—then you will have trouble with this kind of trust.

You easily trust people with whom you have no intimate partnership. Doctors, teachers, and coaches are easy to trust because you share only a little bit of yourself with them. You do not have to open your heart completely to them. But a lifelong bonded relationship requires more. It requires heart-to-heart intimacy. To open your heart allows someone to see you as you really are: to see your personal history, your wounds, your flaws, your immaturities, your habits, and your sins. Transparency like this is a great risk unless you are completely innocent. Children have no trouble with intimacy until the first time their heart is wounded and trust is broken. To make your relationship a happy one, you must find a partner you can trust, and who will trust you with their heart in the same way, to the same depth. You are with the wrong person if you do not trust them intimately!

We withhold trust when we avoid conversations about intimate things. By this, I'm not talking about sensual or sexual conversations. Intimate discussions include how you feel about yourself, your hopes and dreams, your greatest fears, your weaknesses, and your childhood wounds. We date in order to build trust with each other like this. Courtship continues to build trust in additional areas. Any other reason to date is vain and pointless.

In his book, *I Kissed Dating Goodbye,* Josh Harris describes intimacy as the "reward for commitment."[15] Commitment and intimacy belong together. But intimacy without commitment brings heartbreak.

Your open-hearted trust must be protected by your partner. That protection is the beginning of commitment.

How can a woman trust her male partner? How can she ever abandon her fears and lose her control to follow his lead? This was the question facing Kate Mosley in the movie, *The Cutting Edge.*[16] Kate and former hockey star Doug Dorsey became figure skating teammates, even though they didn't like each other. But Kate had not yet captured first place and the coveted Olympic gold medal. She could not place her full trust in her male partners. In figure skating, that trust meant complete surrender to his lifts and throws during competition. Trust was too dangerous for Kate! Doug accused her of holding back with him and her former male skating partners. Kate confessed, knowing her lack of trust was exposed. In the moments before their final Olympic performance together, Kate and Doug spoke words of love to one another for the first time. His love gave her the trust she needed for a breathtaking Olympic performance.

Most of us have been let down by someone we trusted. The other person failed to meet our needs or our expectations. We judged them to be insufficient. After a disappointment, we act with more caution, more control. We remain tense so we are not caught off guard by the unexpected.

Commitment to a bonded relationship requires trust with abandon. Trust withheld, conditional trust, or partial trust with boundaries will be like cold water on the fires of passion. The relationship becomes a disappointment. In athletics, trust is earned by practice and per-formance. Each member takes risks to win. Partners in an intimate relationship also must take risks to trust.

CHAPTER NINETEEN

THE SERVANT'S HEART—HOW GOD USES RELATIONSHIPS

Hosea was a man who lived about 715 years before Christ. In this story, we learn how passionate God Himself is about relationship with His people. Today, all believers in Jesus Christ are invited into that passionate relationship as part of the family of God. Understanding why God made you is fundamental to understanding how to commit to a lifelong bonded relationship. It is a sad, heartbreaking fact that so many young men and women make the mistake of choosing a relationship that can only hurt them. Many books, including this one, have been published to offer the hope that good relationships can be found by individuals willing to make the extra effort to follow the original design for happiness.

You will remember from Chapter One that God *created* Adam and Eve. As their Father, He made the decision that they belonged together. They had no choice in choosing their partners. For many generations, fathers chose marriage partners for their children. The story of Isaac and Rebecca is a romantic read in the book of Genesis.

While I will not suggest that we return to that method of choosing a mate, I can offer encouragement to single men and women longing for a partner. Fathers like myself understand the importance of preparing their sons and daughters for their future relationships. I consider it a most significant facet of my destiny to train my five sons to be men of integrity, able to protect a young woman's precious heart, capable of lifelong commitment to her and to God, even in the face of hardships. I have often jokingly said to other parents that I was searching for a family of five well-trained girls to cut a deal on behalf of my sons. I would interview the girls' parents, each of the daughters, and then suggest to the girls' father my choice for the matches. He and I would do our best to protect the needs of our sons and daughters to assure their long-term happiness.

Now, don't close the book. I know it's not going to happen that way. But there are many parents concerned for the heartbreaks awaiting their children who do not ask for advice.

Let's go back to Hosea. God called him to demonstrate by his life how the Israelites had been unfaithful to their bonded relationship with God.

> When the Lord began to speak through Hosea, the Lord said to him, "Go, take to yourself an adulterous wife and children of unfaithfulness, because the land is guilty of the vilest adultery in departing from the Lord.
>
> (Hosea 1:2)

How do you think Hosea felt when he received *that* word from the Lord? Was he so pious that he didn't care if his wife was unfaithful? Did she come to him with emotional handicaps? Absolutely! The Bible says she took off to see other men, yet the Lord said to Hosea, "Go show your love to your wife again" (Hosea 3:1–2). Hosea never once complained to God. He accepted his role to love and forgive an unfaithful woman, because through the example of Hosea's life, God described His love and faithfulness to an unfaithful nation.

You would think this was the story of a disastrous marriage, but in this book of the Bible we find some of the most beautiful words of love ever written. In fact, listen to the passion in the next passage of scripture where God is so excited that He speaks as both the bride and groom, with great hope for the fulfillment of the relationship. First, speaking as the groom:

> Therefore, behold, I will allure her and bring her into the wilderness, and speak comfortably unto her. And I will give her her vineyards from thence, and the valley of Achor for a door of hope: and she shall sing there, as in the days of her youth, and as in the day when she came up out of the land of Egypt. And it shall be at that day, saith the Lord, that thou shalt call me Ishi [my husband]; and shalt call me no more Baali, [my master] . . . And I will betroth

> thee unto me forever: yea, I will betroth thee unto me in righteousness, and in judgment, and in lovingkindness, and in mercies. I will even betroth thee unto me in faithfulness: and thou shalt know the Lord.
>
> (Hosea 2:14–16, 19–20 KJV)

Then, speaking as the bride:

> Come, and let us return unto the Lord: for he hath torn, and he will heal us; he hath smitten, and he will bind us up. After two days he will revive us: in the third day he will raise us up, and we shall live in his sight. Then shall we know, if we follow on to know the Lord: his going forth is prepared as the morning; and he shall come unto us as the rain, as the latter and former rain unto the earth.
>
> (Hosea 6:1–3 KJV)

Finally, speaking again as the groom:

> O Ephraim, what shall I do unto thee? O Judah, what shall I do unto thee? For your goodness is as a morning cloud, and as the early dew it goeth away.
>
> (Hosea 6:4 KJV)

In these words, God revealed the longing of His heart for a deep bonded relationship with His people. It sounds like God Almighty is crying out with passion for His bride. You and I have this as a model of what a marriage relationship can be!

God is passionate about relationships! He designed man and woman to experience in each other something that goes far beyond companionship, affection, and intimacy. The lifetime commitment a couple enjoys now is like training wheels for an eternal commitment with Jesus Christ after our death. Why do you think God redeemed His people? He could have repeated creation and given up on us with our fallen, sinful natures. But He loved us from the beginning. He longs for an intimate everlasting bonded relationship with us.

So do you really want to try to form relationships without knowing God? Your chances of success are only 50/50. This is important because, when we grasp the eternal significance of bonded love, we have a much greater capacity to love our earthly mate. The bond we have with our human mate becomes much stronger. We are free to love unconditionally. Failure is unthinkable.

The principle of faithfulness is beautifully described in a book by Eric and Leslie Ludy called *When God Writes Your Love Story.*[17] Right in the middle of that book, they discuss the joys of those who decided to be faithful to their future spouse even before they met. They even cite examples of parents who prayed for their children's future spouses long before they met each other. I hope you see that better relationships than you ever imagined await you, if you will follow good advice. Your relationships have a purpose!

CHAPTER TWENTY

THE REDEMPTIVE TEST—HOW DO YOU KNOW WHAT IS RIGHT?

The first sentence of Rick Warren's best selling book, *The Purpose Driven Life,* is this: "It's not about you."[18] Back in Chapter One, I made the point that love makes no sense without God as its designer. If you can accept that principle, then you need to take one more step to understand what makes a relationship good— you are here for God's purpose, not for yourself alone. You will find happiness in all facets of life when you agree with His purpose about why He put you here. Your career, talents, strengths, and yes, your relationships have purpose beyond yourself. Great men and women are often preceded by great parents and grandparents. God takes His time arranging destinies.

Recognizing your purpose in life is, for many people, a complete shift from self-centered purposes to God's purposes. This level of maturity often comes at the price of personal brokenness. Having your own way often results in a broken heart or a deflated ego. Until you understand this, the painful cycle will repeat.

Our lifestyles of fast food, cell phones, winning the lottery, drive-through banking, and high-speed internet have deprived us of the virtue of patience. Wisdom, peace, and relationships are not like that.

But you really want an answer to the question, "How do I know this relationship is right for me?" You must ask this in the context of purpose. The stakes are very high when a lifetime commitment is on the line. It takes two people of integrity, each with a servant's heart, to forge a bonded relationship that lasts a lifetime.

So how should a person go forward? Start by applying the principle I call the "redemptive test." You simply answer this question from your heart with absolute honesty: does this person I want to be with bring any redemptive value to my life? In other words, will you be a better person when bonded to this individual? Tell yourself why. Your happiness does not come to you any other way.

The redemptive test may be used to judge any part of our lives against God's standards in the Scriptures. It is not necessary that you be an accomplished scholar of the Scriptures to learn how to apply the test, because God says He will write His law upon our hearts. Start by asking the question with an open heart. Once you are able to do that, you will hear the still small voice of God as His Holy Spirit quickens you with the truth.

So when judging a potential relationship, ask yourself questions like these: Does this person's character bring out the best in me? Will his (or her) involvement in my life help me to overcome my weak areas? You need to be honest about your weak areas. Remember Sapphira? Peter gave her one last chance to repent, but as a consequence for repeating her husband's lie, she too died an early death without integrity.

Also ask yourself: Does this person's life goals come from a servant's heart or a lifestyle of self-indulgence? Self-indulgence is the hallmark of pride and vanity. These people never reach fulfillment. They strive constantly, but never find contentment.

Does this relationship interfere with something important to you? How does it fit with your own understanding of your destiny? The redemptive test will yield answers that are in concert with God's plan for you. Redemption involves the renewing of your mind, as well as the purging of your conscience. "Do not conform any longer to the pattern of this world, but be transformed by the renewing of your mind" (Rom. 12:2). A renewed mind can understand God's plan. A purged conscience can find contentment and peace. It takes both to trust your bonded partner. Love is built upon such foundational principles. Biochemistry does not make a relationship last; rather, it takes a disciplined heart, fulfilling its God-ordained destiny!

CHAPTER TWENTY-ONE

WHY BONDED RELATIONSHIPS FAIL

Quit, split, and divorce! It seems to affect everybody you know. What has gone wrong? There are as many reasons for broken relationships as there are marriages that break up. But just as common are couples resigned to live in functional but unhappy marriages.

You won't find statistics about unhappiness, but you will observe the stress and strife on their faces if you watch these couples interact with each other. It's even more obvious when they are rarely seen together. You need not hear what they say to each other to see the unhappy body language. These couples remain together for the sake of their children or for other reasons, but they have no joy in each other. They have nowhere else to go, so they live at opposite ends of the same house. Their brief discussions cover the weather, the budget, their schedules, and the transportation needs of their children. Family time is rare. Each has a lowered self-esteem. Neither has the motivation to become intimate, nor the strength to try something new, like counseling. In their weakened state of relationship, they even fail to recognize the external effects of an enemy between them, adding further depressing thoughts of hopelessness. This enemy, of course, is the Satan of the Bible.

Jesus Christ redeems people who choose to accept His gift. But Satan's mission is to spread misery. He whispers thoughts of hopelessness and despair to those already unhappy. He tries to destroy families because the family is a model of Christ's church. He hates that model. A man or woman without a relationship with God is completely blind to this influence, and does not know that healing of the relationship is possible.

A divorce leaves little hope for reconciliation. But unhappy couples that remain together can be revived. Each must want to change or nothing will happen. Joy is a by-product of love. It is better than simple contentment, better than an arms-length peace, and better than mere functional commitment. Remember, love is a decision. A person of integrity does not make a vow of unconditional love lightly, and will be faithful even without joy. But joy can be recovered.

No couple expects to come to this place of unhappiness when they begin life together. But character flaws, character handicaps, immaturity, selfishness, and lack of relationship training eventually become issues that can separate two people in a relationship.

Many marriages fail because couples have no idea what to do when their contentions get serious. Usually, they blame the other person and shift the blame away from themselves. But that only ignites more conflict! In the Biblical account of the first sin, Adam blamed Eve, and Eve blamed the serpent. Neither took responsibility for what they did. Nothing good comes from blame-shifting!

In his book, *Love and Respect,* author Emerson Eggerichs describes how a couple can go around and around in a cycle of strife.[19] He calls it the "crazy cycle" because it is endless until someone learns to stop giving the same old response to the same old aggravation. The "crazy cycle" brings people to the brink of divorce, because they see no escape from unhappy confrontation in their relationship. Dr. Eggerichs's *Love and Respect* is not only a superb source of remedial help for couples in trouble, but it is well worth reading by single men and women who want to know how to preserve a relationship.

My answer to the question, "Why do bonded relationships fail?" is this: Bonded relationships fail when couples ignore God's plan for redemption, when they lack training in conflict resolution, when they fail to get help early, and when they lack integrity.

Electronic matchmaking, which asserts that happiness comes to two people well-matched for compatibility, does not provide a sufficient foundation for lifelong, unconditional commitment. Conflict is a fact of real life. Every well-matched couple will ride on Dr. Eggerichs's "crazy cycle" simply because men and women think differently. Every highly compatible couple will come under the influence of Satan's destructive activity against families, whether they know it or not.

Our present population, from post-WWII baby boomers to Generation X and Generation Y, has seen the greatest increase ever in methods of instant self-gratification. They drive the speed limit plus 10, become enraged by other drivers, need to be constantly wired to music, sports, and instant messages, seek abortions on demand after unsafe sex, pay for next day shipping, and grow up at 13. Their credit cards are maxed-out; they believe the next lottery will be their big chance; they salt the roads to melt snow faster; and they coach junior sports teams on Sundays. Ice time is at 5:30 AM; away games are in the next state; video rentals are mailed twice a week. We hear, "Are we there yet?" after only 15 minutes on the road; we pay our bills instantly online; and ATM machines are open 24/7.

Whatever happened to virtuous patience? Impatience and instant gratification are so universal that we don't remember anything different. Relationships require patience. Patience precedes peace in the home. Yet everything around us screams, "Get it now!" The most famous text in the Bible defining love begins with "Love is patient . . ." (1 Cor. 13:4). There is a reason for that. Patience makes way for conflict resolution.

Reasons why bonded relationships fail become clear when we rewrite the 1 Corinthians text in the negative, like this:

> Broken relationships lack patience, ignore kindness, and are envious, boastful and proud. The partners in a relationship become rude toward one another, seeking only fulfillment of their own needs. They are easily angered, remembering everything their partners did that hurt them, and bringing up that history in every argument. A broken relationship delights in getting even, and doesn't want to hear the truth. A broken relationship no longer protects, no longer trusts, no longer hopes, and is not willing to persevere through tough times. A broken relationship never succeeds.

CHAPTER TWENTY-TWO

RESPECT VERSUS LOVE

All men need to be respected. All women need to be loved. These distinct needs reflect the differences in emotional wiring between men and women. This doesn't mean that men don't need love, or women don't need respect. We each need both, but we prioritize these needs differently in our lives.

Men need respect like they need oxygen. As oxygen revitalizes his body, respect revitalizes his soul. Both are essential for a healthy life. Respect is about who he is. It is appreciation, honor, esteem, and recognition. Respect appreciates what he does, honors him for his achievements, esteems him for good character, and recognizes him for the man he is. Without respect a man cannot lead, has no courage, and does little to protect. His self-confidence is suffocated. He loses his self-esteem. He becomes a loner. He cannot love.

Therefore, a woman needs to learn how to respect her man. Respect keeps him emotionally balanced and able to meet her needs. He would rather be respected than loved, if he had to make a choice.[20] He is wired that way. The fastest way for a woman to end a relationship is to withhold respect from her partner. He will lose interest, no longer care, and separate.

Women need love like they need water. As water satisfies a woman's thirst, love fulfills her longing to be connected. Love is not just a romantic feeling, even though the movies make it look like that. Love is also more than protection and security.

The defining characteristics of love, quoted previously, need to be repeated here:

> Love is patient, love is kind. It does not envy [that means it's not jealous], it does not boast, it is not proud. It is not rude, it is not self-seeking, it is not easily angered, it keeps

no record of wrongs. Love does not delight in evil but rejoices with the truth. It always protects, always trusts, always hopes, always perseveres.

(1 Cor. 13:4)

Those attributes of love make it safe to be connected. The heart-to-heart bond of a relationship is open because love always trusts, always hopes, always works it through (perseveres) and always protects. This is nurturing, and it describes how women are wired emotionally.

So now we see that respect describes who we are with appreciation, honor, and esteem. And we show love by: practicing patience and kindness; not being jealous, proud, rude, or selfish;, being slow to anger; keeping no record of wrong-doing; not delighting in evil, but rejoicing in truth; always protecting, trusting, hoping, and trying.

Men who love will be respected. Can you understand why some men are not respected? Is it because they don't behave with love? Suppose someone is rude to you by calling you names. Do you then respect him? Suppose someone does not trust you? Do you respect him?

In order to earn respect, a man must behave with love! In order to be loved, a woman must offer her respect.[21] This does not come naturally. We need to learn how to meet each other's needs in this way.

Let's look at two men in the Bible. One was worthy of respect while the other was not. In Genesis 3:6, the Bible says Adam was with Eve when she decided to eat the forbidden fruit. Do we respect Adam for his role in this event? No, we don't! Adam failed to speak up. He failed to protect his wife from the deceiving serpent. Thus, he failed in love according to 1 Corinthians 13. Even though Adam was given a lot of responsibility by God, he is not worthy of our respect because he said nothing about eating the forbidden fruit. In fact, we never use Adam as an example of a man worthy of respect.

In the Bible, we read that Noah "found favor in the eyes of the Lord" (Gen. 6:8). Noah persevered to complete the ark while the people around him became ever more wicked in the eyes of the Lord. "Noah was a righteous man" (Gen. 6:9). We have great respect for Noah because he did not delight in evil, he always trusted God, he always hoped in God, and he kept trying to finish the ark in the spirit of 1 Corinthians 13.

CHAPTER TWENTY-THREE
GIVE AND TAKE

Every established relationship requires times of give and take. But in the beginning of a relationship, a young couple's taking from each other and giving to one another can be a big source of misunderstanding. A young man and woman seeking to form long-term relationship must not overextend this giving and taking. Broken hearts and unhappy relationships start because of unguarded giving and taking.

Let me explain it this way. Romance and chemistry are so thrilling that we all too quickly imagine ourselves moving to the next level of the relationship. Not only does the princess hope her prince will call, but she wants him to stay . . . forever. She dreams of his ever-after commitment to protect and cherish her. She quite willingly gives her heart to her prince even before he has earned her love. She is carried away by the thought of her dream coming true.

The prince, meanwhile, feels strong and manly because he has pursued a princess and found her to be captivating. He feels exhilarated by her attention, respected, honored, and invincible!

And so, both the prince and the princess have feelings beyond the moment. They are "falling in love." He tells her he wants to see her again. She waits for his parting kiss.

But she has already given too much. He has taken more than he should. He lived that moment to its fullest. Tomorrow he would have to return to the battle. Commitment was out of the question. He did not know her heart was fully exposed and unguarded. He did not know she needed that kind of protection.

Many a young man does not understand how to protect a woman's heart. He takes too much from her by allowing commitment to be inferred from his words, his kiss, and his desire to see her again. The word "inferred" means that the hearer of the words expected something that was not explicitly stated by the speaker. In other words, she presumed things he did not say. Suppose a man discusses with a woman his plan to build a house and have a garden someday. While he may be simply sharing some of his hopes and dreams, she may "infer" that he is thinking about settling down with *her*. After all, he is telling *her* these things about himself. Her whole being is hanging on the continuation of the relationship. She will infer that his commitment to her is imminent because of their conversations. This is how easily a man can be misunderstood.

He compartmentalizes his experience while he attends to other matters in his life. She, on the other hand, is totally involved. He holds fond memories, but does not need the commitment now. She cries; he can't understand. She has given too much. In his ignorance, he has taken from her much more than he should have.

The majority of young men do not yet understand the things that are important to women. Because the genders are wired differently, a woman's expectations combined with a man's intentions often become a recipe for a broken heart. Anytime he speaks to her about his plans for the future, she becomes vulnerable to false expectations. Anytime he becomes intimate with his words, his kiss, or his affections, she senses that he belongs exclusively to her. While he can quickly move on to another issue, she remains behind, locked in her dreams of being together. Broken hearts abound because he doesn't understand he has captivated her heart.

Before a man begins a romantic relationship with a woman, he must learn how to protect her heart. He learns this from his sisters. The writers of the New Testament used two Greek words for relationship: *agape* and *phileo*. Both are translated in English as "love." *Agape* means the unconditional and self-sacrificing love of a spouse, while *phileo* means brotherly love, as in friendly affection.

Men and women need to learn the skill of friendly affection before romance. Beyond our blood relationships of brothers, sisters, and cousins, we also have opportunities to learn in youth groups, summer camps, and other supervised youth activities. We emphasize this because, in prior generations, it was normal to separate boys from girls in every way. The baby boomer generation grew up with no supervised training in brotherly love for the opposite gender. We were completely separated in Boy Scouts and Girl Scouts, boys' schools and girls' schools, all-male colleges and all-female colleges. We never learned how each gender thinks about things—how the other sex is wired. Our casual relationships were few and far between.

While a man must protect the heart of a woman in a relationship, she also has a protective role to fulfill. She must learn to honor his uncontrollable weakness for visual stimulation. Her style of clothing will cause him to infer expectations, just as his way of talking affects her heart. He will not be able to see beauty within her if she plays to his visual obsession. He will not want to think about the future if the present is too enticing. She is giving away too much. Men usually do only one thing at a time. If she holds his attention with tight clothing emphasizing her curves, he will be too distracted to have any relationship-building conversation. His ego will be in overdrive. He will develop an appetite for more of a physical relationship.

Discounting these factors and going along with the "everybody's doing it" attitude will only get you the same results: 50% of marriages ending in divorce, heartbreak, and loneliness.

Everyone has choices in life. Every choice you make, no matter how small, leads you toward either happiness or heartbreak. Heartbreak is easy. If you think like everyone else and behave with no personal dignity or integrity, you'll get what everyone else gets. But now you know how to make better choices.

There is no shame in dreaming big dreams. God designed relationships to be very good, fulfilling, lifelong experiences. And if you think you'll never find your prince or princess, let me offer this hope. The very last verse in the Old Testament includes this phrase; "He will turn the hearts of the fathers to their children, and the hearts of the children to their fathers" (Malachi 4:6). Many fathers are stepping up to their responsibility to teach their children about life and relationships. They understand their destiny to make a difference for the next generation . . . your generation. Their sons and daughters are being prepared to meet you with integrity and lifelong bonded commitment. Single, eligible young men and women of integrity are out there, if only you will be patient.

CHAPTER TWENTY-FOUR

HAPPY EVER AFTER

You can choose to live "happily-ever-after." You were created for someone, but you will only recognize the right person if you learn what to look for. You don't have to wait for good things to happen in your life. You can begin right now with what you have to prepare for the relationship of your dreams. Your hope will become a source of happiness as you work toward your dream. Hope even makes you more attractive. The fundamental ideas should now be clear. You must:

1. Understand God's design for a long-term bonded relationship between a man and a woman
2. Know yourself, your character strengths and weaknesses, and your particular hopes and dreams
3. Recognize that long-term relationships will not be likely to succeed without God's help
4. Have a personal relationship with God before you choose your mate for life
5. Build the relationship with your intended mate slowly, involving others for accountability and guidance
6. Remain patient as you both mature and understand the concept of lifelong commitment
7. Not give your heart or affections away before the proper time
8. Fulfill your adult responsibilities, like schooling and career, before you take on the adult commitment of wedding vows

There are excellent books available that provide more specific guidance on dating, purity, communication, courtship, and marriage itself. Let me remind you again of the blessings you stand to gain from proper preparation for your special relationship: peace and contentment in your home; strong commitment from your spouse, even in difficult times; personal happiness from several sources, including your spouse, your children, and your work all in balance; love that has the ability to rekindle lost passion; and the satisfaction of finding your destiny in life.

Your happiness comes from understanding your purpose, not from getting what you want. When you learn why you are here and accept your God-given roles, you will find complete freedom from inner strife. After you meet God personally through Jesus Christ, you are never alone. He has never broken up with anyone, never walked out on anyone, never reacted with violence, never lost interest in anyone, and never given up on a relationship. He has never withheld forgiveness, never made a bad choice, never changed His mind, and never become anything less than He purposed to be. He defines the model person in perfect relationship, and he has an intended purpose in defining who you are to be.

You can choose to ignore these facts, be independent and in charge of your own life, resist accountability, and strive to fulfill your own needs in the way you see fit. But isn't that what everybody else is doing? And we know at least half of them are unhappy.

Love is the hardest subject to learn when we have not been taught how to love. If you grew up in a broken home, you have an emotional handicap to overcome because you have not seen first hand how real love endures. Your experience has shown you that love fails, and that commitments are not strong bonds. But you can make a difference for yourself by learning to recognize the distinguishing characteristics of a love that lasts. You can make better choices. You can find people who know what it takes, and who can tell you how to prepare.

The biggest obstacle for most people is the lack of selection of potential partners. Their circle of friends and acquaintances is small. They don't know where to find a person with the high qualities they cherish. They fear they never will find someone, and they fear failure simply because they experience loneliness. Loneliness leads to impatience, and impatience causes people to give up their dreams and accept less. But God created you to make someone else happy, and God created someone just for you.

ENDNOTES

Chapter Two

1. Based upon the Broad Foundations Laid Down by Noah Webster, Webster's New Twentieth Century Dictionary of the English Language Unabridged (New York, NY: Rockville House Publishers, Inc., 1952), 1434.

2. Dr. Neil Clark Warren, *Falling in Love for all the Right Reasons,* (Brentwood, TN: Center Street, 2005), 36.

3. Dr. Neil Clark Warren, *Falling in Love for all the Right Reasons*, (Brentwood, TN: Center Street, 2005), 55.

Chapter Eight

4. Based upon the Broad Foundations Laid Down by Noah Webster, Webster's New Twentieth Century Dictionary of the English Language Unabridged (New York, NY: Rockville House Publishers, Inc., 1952), 904.

Chapter Nine

5. John Eldredge, *Wild at Heart: Discovering the Secret to a Man's Soul* (Nashville, TN: Thomas Nelson, Inc., 2006), 59.

Chapter Ten

6. Columbia Pictures (production company), *First Knight*, Sony Pictures Studio, VHS, 1996.

Chapter Eleven

7. Based upon the Broad Foundations Laid Down by Noah Webster, Webster's New Twentieth Century Dictionary of the English Language Unabridged (New York, NY: Rockville House Publishers, Inc., 1952), 1351.

8. The witness's oath (common usage).

9. Based upon the Broad Foundations Laid Down by Noah Webster, Webster's New Twentieth Century Dictionary of the English Language Unabridged (New York, NY: Rockville House Publishers, Inc., 1952), 1151.

10. Traditional wedding vow (common usage).

11. Based upon the Broad Foundations Laid Down by Noah Webster, Webster's New Twentieth Century Dictionary of the English Language Unabridged (New York, NY: Rockville House Publishers, Inc., 1952), 1929.

12. Based upon the Broad Foundations Laid Down by Noah Webster, Webster's New Twentieth Century Dictionary of the English Language Unabridged (New York, NY: Rockville House Publishers, Inc., 1952), 170.

Chapter Twelve

13. Josh Harris, *I Kissed Dating Goodbye* (Colorado Springs, CO: The WaterBrook Multnomah Publishing Group, 2003), 28.

Chapter Seventeen

14. Merlin Carothers, *Power in Praise* (Gainesville, FL: Bridge-Logos Publishers, 1993).

Chapter Eighteen

15. Josh Harris, *I Kissed Dating Goodbye* (Colorado Springs, CO: The WaterBrook Multnomah Publishing Group, 2003), 28.

16. MGM, *The Cutting Edge*, DVD 2001.

Chapter Nineteen

17. Eric and Leslie Ludy, *When God Writes Your Love Story: The Ultimate Approach to Guy/Girl Relationships* (Colorado Springs, CO: The WaterBrook Multnomah Publishing Group, 2004), 127.

Chapter Twenty

18. Rick Warren, *The Purpose Driven Life: What on Earth Am I Here For?* (Grand Rapids, MI: Zondervan, 2002), 17.

Chapter Twenty-one

19. Emerson Eggerichs, *Love & Respect: The Love She Most Desires; The Respect He Desperately Needs* (Nashville: Thomas Nelson, Inc., 2004), 16.

Chapter Twenty-two

20. Shaunti Feldhahn, *For Women Only: What You Need to Know about the Inner Lives of Men* (Colorado Springs, CO: The WaterBrook Multnomah Publishing Group, 2004), 22.

21. Emerson Eggerichs, *Love & Respect: The Love She Most Desires; The Respect He Desperately Needs* (Nashville: Thomas Nelson, Inc., 2004), 113.